AGING IN AND OUT
OF PLACE

Christina Clark-Kazak

AGING IN AND OUT OF PLACE

Lived Experiences of
Forced Migration Across
the Life Course

**The Forced Migration
Studies Collection**

Collection Editors

T. Alexander Aleinikoff &

Laura Hammond

For Martyn and Margaret Clark, who inspired thousands of young people to challenge societally imposed age limits.

First published in 2024 by Lived Places Publishing

British Library Cataloguing in Publication Data
A CIP record for this book is available from the British Library

ISBN: 9781915734594 (pbk)
ISBN: 9781915734600 (ePDF)
ISBN: 9781915734617 (ePUB)

Cover design by Fiachra McCarthy
Book design by Rachel Trolove of Twin Trail Design
Typeset by Newgen Publishing UK

Lived Places Publishing
Long Island
New York 11789

www.livedplacespublishing.com

Abstract

Tracing the lived experiences of childhood, youth, adulthood, and old age in forced migration contexts, *Aging In and Out of Place* explores how social age as an identity marker changes over time, space, and place. By centering stories of displacement in Canada, the US, Germany, the UK, and Australia, this book analyzes the impact of national and international policies and their engagement with individual and collective identity markers, including age, gender, sexual orientation, disability, race, and religion. Providing innovative insights into the underexplored area of social age in forced migration research, policy and practice, *Aging In and Out of Place* is ideal reading for students of interdisciplinary courses including Forced Migration and Refugee Studies, Childhood Studies, Development Studies, and Gerontology, as well as policy makers.

Keywords

aging, displacement, mobility, childhood, family, identity, youth, gerontology, policy

Contents

Learning objectives

By the end of this book, readers should be able to:

- Critically analyze, and explain, the socially constructed nature of aging in diverse migration contexts.
- Understand how migration experiences impact how people experience different stages of the life course.
- Provide examples of lived experiences of aging in different migration contexts.
- Identify relevant resources for further research, practice, and policymaking.

1
Introduction to social age and forced migration

This book is about the lived experiences of people who are born, grow up, transition to adulthood, age, and die in forced migration contexts. While much of the policy, media, and research focuses on one age category—like refugee children—*Aging In and Out of Place* instead analyzes the trajectories and relationships of human beings migrating across the life course. My intent is to show how forced migration is a human phenomenon, involving and impacting people in different stages of life and in intergenerational families, households, and communities. While the book covers many different aspects of aging from cradle to grave[1] in forced migration contexts, it is not exhaustive. Rather, by highlighting the richness of a comprehensive approach to both social age and forced migration, I hope to inspire more holistic discussions, research, policy, and programming.

A social age approach

This book takes as its point of departure the idea that the aging process is both a biological fact of life, but also socially constructed in particular times and places. A baby is obviously physically, cognitively, and emotionally different than an older child or an adult. But the meanings attached to human development and the socially acceptable roles at different stages of the life course vary significantly across different cultures, religions, and communities. Historians have also shown how the social construction of aging has varied across time (Cunningham, 1995; Burgard, 2021).

I use the concept of "social age" to describe these socially constructed aspects of the human development and aging processes. Social age refers to the localized, social meanings and roles ascribed to different stages of the life course (Clark-Kazak, 2009b). Social age also encompasses power relations embedded in intergenerational relationships (Clark-Kazak, 2013). For example, in societies that venerate old age and equate "elders" with wisdom, children may be socially defined as those who "don't reason" or "don't understand" (Clark-Kazak, 2011, p. 9). Taking a relational approach to aging allows for an analytical process that acknowledges the intersection of social age with other power relations.

Black feminist Kimberlé Crenshaw developed the concept of intersectionality as a metaphor to show how power structures and relationships overlap (Crenshaw, 1989). In this book, we will think about how social age intersects with other factors like gender, sexual orientation, (dis)ability, class, racialization, religion, ethnicity, and migration status to understand diverse experiences of aging in forced migration contexts. In other words, a Black Muslim Somali woman who arrived in Canada as a refugee and does not qualify for Canadian Pension Plan payments will have a different experience of old age than a White, Christian,

Canadian-born man who has access to both private and public pensions.

Limitations to the dominant chronological approach to measuring age

In cultures ordered by chronometric time, chronological age is the dominant way of measuring age. This has spilled over into western medicine, psychology (Rogoff, 1991), education (Veraksa and Pramling Samuelsson, 2022), and law (Bhabha, 2009; Crock and Martin, 2018). International legal instruments predominantly refer to chronological age. For example, the Convention on the Rights of the Child—the most widely ratified human rights treaty in the world—defines a child as "every human being below the age of eighteen years unless under the law applicable to the child, majority is attained earlier" (article 1).

While chronological age is therefore sometimes believed to be a "universal" and "neutral" measure, it is insufficient as the sole measurement of aging in migration contexts for three key reasons. First, as will be discussed in more detail in Chapter 2, people in contexts of migration do not necessarily know, or have documents to prove, their chronological age. Because many international agencies and governments rely on chronological age to administer programs and determine eligibility for services and access to rights, this lack of documentation poses practical problems. As a result, many western liberal democracies have invested significant resources and political capital into age assessments through dental, bone density or sexual maturity measurements (Sypek *et al.*, 2016), despite critiques of their accuracy and ethics.

Because of the margin of error of +/- 3 years and the inability of age-disputed young people to freely consent to age assessments (Silverman, 2016), some researchers have gone as far as to call them "junk science" (Noll, 2016).

Second, in migration contexts, social and physical markers may be as, if not more, important than chronological age to determine relationships across the life course. Many cultures and religions practice rites of passage that determine when one is considered to be an adult. Puberty is a biological characteristic that signifies adulthood in many cultures, particularly once a person is physically able to bear children. Similarly, physical changes like menopause and greying hair may be interpreted as the beginning of old age. Other socially significant events like marriage and parenthood may signal a transition from youth to adulthood, as will be explored in greater detail in Chapter 3.

Third, chronological age is itself socially constructed, made meaningful in contexts ordered by chronometric time, where there is significant difference of opinion about the age that is appropriate for voting, driving, marriage, engaging in consensual sex, remunerated work, retirement, etc. This shows that chronological age cut-offs, while administratively efficient, are arbitrary and not as neutral as implied in legal and policy documents. Indeed, even within the same immigration law, there may be different chronological ages defining "children" (Clark-Kazak, 2025).

Life course approach

This is not to suggest that the chronological passage of time is completely irrelevant to studying aging. Rather, this book is interested in aging across the life course precisely because the passage of time has different socially significant meanings. The life course approach, combined with the social age analysis developed above, is concerned with how chronometric time is made meaningful in people's lives, rather than assuming that chronological age tells the whole story.

The life course approach analyzes aging through a series of transitions or life events, which people pass through over time (Kulu and Milewski, 2007). These socially significant transitions and events are made meaningful within particular social relationships and geographic and temporal contexts (Giele and Elder, 1998). Migration research is interested in how life course decisions, such as marriage, family planning, or retirement, influence migration decisions and vice versa (Gardner, 2009, 2021). In this way, the chronological and historical passage of time are mapped onto both aging and migration. We will return to the temporal nature of migration and aging in the last chapter.

What is forced migration?

Migration refers to the movement of people. It has been part of human history since the beginning of time. However, in the contemporary context of sovereign states, governments are increasing concerned with "managing" and categorizing migration. Under international law and policy, and domestic legislation, there is generally a distinction between "forced" and "voluntary" migration. Forced migration describes situations where people are driven from their homes due to violence, persecution, human rights abuses, or environmental degradation. Voluntary migration occurs when people choose to move for family, work, or education purposes. Forced migration is the primary focus of this book.

Of course, in reality, this forced-voluntary binary is not clearcut. Even people who are forced to leave make decisions about when to flee, where to go, and how to move. Similarly, people who migrate for family, work, or educational purposes may be constrained by financial or social pressures. A person's immigration status may also change. For example, an Afghan young woman studying in Australia as an international student may have claimed refugee status after the Taliban retook control and banned women from studying and working. Or an asylum seeker in the US may marry a US citizen, providing a pathway to permanent residency through marriage sponsorship.

While the emphasis of forced migration often is on movement, it also includes immobility (Bélanger and Silvey, 2020). People may be trapped behind closed borders, like Palestinians who cannot leave Gaza. Or people may initially be displaced across a border, but then be confined within refugee camps or detention centers or face limited access to services and opportunities because of precarious migration status. Therefore, in this book, I include a variety of legal statuses under the umbrella term "forced migration". *Aging In and Out of Place* follows the life course experiences of refugees, resettled refugees who may arrive in a new country as permanent residents, asylum seekers, and people with precarious status.

It is important to note that most forced migration worldwide occurs within and between countries of the Global South. Table 1.1 below summarizes the numbers of people displaced

Table 1.1 Top source and host countries at end of 2022

Source country	Host country
Syrian Arab Republic (6.5 million)	Iran (3.4 million)
Afghanistan (6.1 million)	Turkey (3.4 million)
Ukraine (5.9 million)	Germany (2.5 million)
	Colombia (2.5 million)
	Pakistan (2.1 million)

Source: UNHCR, 2023a

worldwide as represented in UNHCR statistics at the end of 2023. These data also indicate that 40% of displaced people are children under the age of 18, while only 4% are over the age of 60. Comparing the demographics of displacement with the population in the country of origin shows that fewer people migrate as they age, begging the question of what happens to older people, who are often left behind (HelpAge International, 2024b). We will return to this point in Chapter 5.

While not ignoring the reality of forced migration in lower income countries of the Global South, this book foregrounds the lived experiences of people who have arrived in Canada, the United States, Australia, Germany, and the United Kingdom as resettled refugees, refugee claimants (also called asylum seekers), or irregular migrants. Resettlement is the process by which refugees whom the UN Refugee Agency has been identified as needing protection in a country of asylum are brought permanently to another country. The US, Canada, and Australia have led global resettlement efforts over many years, with some variations depending on the political party in power at any given time.

Asylum is enshrined in international and domestic laws. While everyone has the right to seek asylum, the refugee status determination (RSD) process varies by country. Most of the RSD systems use the refugee definition found in the 1951 UN Convention: a person who fears persecution because of race, religion, nationality, or membership in a particular social group. Germany is a main European destination for asylum seekers and refugees, as shown in Table 1.1.

Finally, there are people who have been forced to leave their countries, but do not fit the narrow definition of the 1951 Convention and/or are not legally entitled to enter another, so have to resort to irregular migration to access precarious protections. Rich countries in the Global North have increasingly developed "architectures of repulsion" (FitzGerald, 2019) to try to keep potential asylum seekers out though visa policies, immigration detention, including in offshore facilities (see Chapter 7), and agreements with other countries. The UK has developed the hostile environment policies, recently codified into law, in a futile attempt to deter irregular migration. The US has the largest undocumented population in the world.

In this book, I have chosen to focus on forced migration to Australia, Canada, the US, the UK, and Germany because of the scale of resettlement and irregular migration, but also because the cultural situation is often very different from forced migrants' countries of origins, posing specific questions about the social construction of aging and family relationships. Moreover, in these rich countries of the Global North, governments should have the resources and capacity to uphold age- and migration-specific rights, but the reality is that sometimes these policies fall short.

Legal and policy approaches to aging and migration

Indeed, the notion of universality of human rights means that any person, anywhere, is supposed to have the same rights and protections. For example, the next chapter highlights some of the rights that apply under the CRC to all children, including children in migration contexts. However, in practice, people in migration contexts have fewer opportunities to exercise their rights than citizens. Hannah Arendt referred to this as "the right to have rights" (1943). As a result, the international community has negotiated specific refugee and migration treaties, as well as the non-binding Global Compacts on migration and refugees. These legal and normative standards contain specific provisions on family unity, health, education, and work, which are intended to protect non-citizens.

The UN agency for refugees (UNHCR) has also developed an age, gender, and diversity policy in recognition of the differential experiences of migration due to intersecting power relations. UNHCR has guidelines on children, including children who are separated from their families (see Chapter 2), and on older refugees (see Chapter 5). Similarly, the International Organization for Migration (IOM) has developed operational guidance on age, gender, diversity, and protection. While imperfect (Clark-Kazak, 2009a; Thomas and Beck, 2010; UNHCR, 2017), these are important starting points to acknowledge how migration processes affect people differently, with age and life course being important factors.

Centering lived experiences through stories

Because of these differential experiences of migration and aging, this book uses stories to illustrate how people navigate dynamic displacement contexts. In contrast to homogenizing and essentializing discourses about "refugees" and "migrants", I seek to amplify the humanity of people who have been displaced from their homes, their communities, and their networks. At the beginning of each chapter, I use the story of one person to illustrate some of the key themes related to aging and migration. These stories are not intended to be representative—they are only one person's experiences among millions. Rather, the point is to demonstrate how borders intersect with people's lives, and how immigration status has significant consequences for important life decisions, like education, marriage, parenthood, and retirement. Some of the people profiled in this book are well known; others are not. Indeed, as a human phenomenon, migration permeates life in both extraordinary and ordinary ways. I wanted the book to show how displacement affects people across the life course, but also in very different life circumstances.

I chose to use stories that were already publicly available in media and other print sources. Researchers in forced migration studies have drawn attention to the problem of over-research, where people who have been displaced feel obligated to tell their story over and over again: to receive legal status, to access services, and to satisfy media and researchers' need for information. I made a conscious decision not to reproduce this harm by insisting on new empirical data for this book. Rather, I repurposed material in existing, publicly available sources, with credit to the original authors, some of whom chose to tell their own stories. If we listen carefully, we can find stories of migration in our families, communities, newspapers, literature, and political discourse. By centering these stories, I encourage readers to proactively and intentionally tune into migration narratives in their own spheres of care.

Conclusion and outline of chapters

This chapter has shown that both migration and aging are human processes that occur within diverse contexts and intersecting power relations. *Aging In and Out of Place* takes a social age approach to highlight life course events in forced migration experiences in countries of resettlement, asylum, and irregular migration in the Global North. Starting with birth, through childhood (Chapter 2), youth (Chapter 3), adulthood (Chapter 4), and old age (Chapter 5), the following chapters provide insights into how forced migration informs key life events. Chapter 6 then turns to the question of changing intergenerational relationships in forced migration. The final chapter sums up ways to think about aging in and out of place through the lens of time.

The purpose of this book is to center aging and life course in discussions of forced migration. While attention in forced migration studies has already been paid to specific age and migration categories, like refugee children, my intent here is to provide a framework for thinking about the intersection of migration and aging in *all* discussions about forced migration. While the scope of the book is broad and cannot cover all aspects of the life course, it provides an entry point for more systematic and holistic discussions about aging when teaching and learning about forced migration.

2
Birth and childhoods in exile

Introduction: Child rights and realities in situations of forced migration

This chapter explores lived experiences of birth and childhood in situations of forced migration. Infants, children, and young people under the age of 18 are accorded specific rights under domestic legislation and the United Nations Convention on the Rights of the Child (CRC)—the most widely ratified international convention. This Convention recognizes that refugee children have the same rights as nationals, including the right to education, health, birth registration, and nationality (article 22). Underpinning the CRC is the best interests of the child principle (article 3). This means that adults and decision-makers should always think about what is best for the child(ren) involved in any situation. In addition, article 12 gives children the right to participate in decisions that affect them. Although all countries except the United States are party to the CRC and should respect children's rights, the reality is that many children and families face structural barriers to realizing their rights in forced migration contexts of discrimination, xenophobia, and limited resources.

Moreover, as discussed in Chapter 1, birth and childhood are socially constructed. This means there are particular social and cultural meanings attached to being born and growing up. The different meanings and expectations related to different phases of the life course are also influenced by gender, religion, ethnicity, racialization, birth order, and other factors. For example, Mayall's (2002, p. 52) research with Muslim children in the UK found that girls had "a clear, gendered understanding of how their life now and in the future should be lived, based on Islamic teaching. … religious observance for girls took up less time, since they did not have to learn the Koran, but only to read it and learn about Islam". Children and their families will also experience birth and childhood differently depending on their positionality within intersecting power relations in their home and host countries (Denov, Mitchell, and Rabiau, 2023). In many cases, children born or growing up in exile straddle different cultural and social expectations about how they should behave and what activities are or are not appropriate for children.

We will turn now to the story of a Syrian family resettled to Canada to illustrate four key points in this chapter. First, the location and registration of birth has significant impacts on the immigration status of the child and their ability to exercise their rights. Second, people giving birth outside their home communities often do not benefit from the same medical access and social and cultural supports as they would if they were in their country of origin. Third, childhood is not a homogeneous experience. It is affected by different cultural, social, and religious practices, as well as an individual's own positionality in relation to racializa-tion, (dis)ability, gender, sexual orientation, birth order, and family circumstances. Finally, while child rights are ostensibly universal, as codified in the CRC, in reality, children are differentially able to exercise their rights because of migration status, geographic location, constrained financial resources, and discrimination.

Birth across borders: Ibtesam Alkarnake's story

In February 2017, Ibtesam Alkarnake, a Syrian woman, made international headlines for giving birth hours after arriving in Canada as a resettled refugee. Ibtesam, her husband and four children aged 5 to 17 had been approved for private sponsorship to Canada[2] through a church in the rural town of Fort McMurray, Alberta. The sponsorship process took over a year, during which time Ibtesam became pregnant. Originally, officials had indi-cated that Ibetsam could not travel, but after the church inter-vened, a health check was performed and she was given the all clear, as her due date was at least a month after the travel date (Kassam, 2017).

On the flight from Jordan, where the family had been living in a refugee camp for five years, Ibtesam's water broke. She didn't tell anyone. "It was the hardest decision for the baby and for the whole family," Ibtesam told CBC News through a translator. "Because I felt I was going to lose the visa. That's why I took the decision" (cited in Thurton, 2017). She endured hours of labor pain during stopovers in Frankfurt and Calgary (Kassam, 2017). Only once she had arrived in Fort McMurray did Ibetsam tell one of the sponsorship volunteers and was rushed to hospital, where she gave birth shortly thereafter (Thurton, 2017).

Ibetsam's baby, Eyad, acquired Canadian citizenship at birth. The other members of the Alkarnake family landed in Canada as permanent residents and could apply for Canadian citizenship after fulfilling language, residency, and knowledge requirements. Eyad has only known childhood and life in Canada, while his sister was born in Jordan and his three older brothers have lived in Syria, Jordan, and Canada. Therefore, the siblings have had different experiences of both childhood and migration—neither of which are homogenous processes (see Chapter 1).

Birth in forced migration contexts

While statistics are difficult to obtain due to gaps in birth registration (see below), the UN Refugee Agency estimates that more than 1.9 million children were born into refugee life between 2018 and 2022 (UNHCR, 2023a). As shown in Eyad's story, where babies are born has a significant impact on the health and safety of their mothers, but also their own immigration status and quality of life.

Refugees and asylum seekers often have difficulty accessing culturally appropriate and medically safe prenatal care, labor and delivery. Many refugee camps do not have adequate obstetrical care infrastructure, resulting in high maternal and infant mortality rates. For the Alkarnake family, this was one reason why Ibetsam travelled so late in her pregnancy: "My wife didn't want to go into labor in the camp," her husband, Medyan Alkarnake said (cited in Thurton, 2017). Research in Rohingya refugee camps in Bangladesh shows that the primary obstacle to accessing adequate maternal care is cost (Parmar *et al.*, 2019). Similarly, resettled refugees and asylum seekers in higher income countries that do not have medical insurance face costly medical bills that can drive them into debt.

Those who do have access to free prenatal, obstetrical and postpartum services may still face discrimination and/or culturally inappropriate care. For example, Elahe Yazdani, an Iranian refugee in Australia, describes giving birth alone in a hospital at the height of the Covid-19 pandemic as "traumatic" and "one of the saddest stories of my life" due to language barriers, discrimination, and lack of informed consent (cited in Burfitt, 2023). Newcomers may also have more difficulty accessing postpartum care and support. For example, in a focus group with Afghan refugees in the US, one woman said, "I was alone too, and I did not have enough experience on how to raise the babies" (cited in Kirkendall and Dutt, 2023).

Due to the significance of geopolitical borders, where a child is born has important implications for their immigration/citizenship status and their documentation as a legal person. Under article 7 of the Convention on the Rights of the Child and article 24, paragraph 2 of the International Covenant on Civil and Political Rights, everyone has the right to birth registration, which provides proof of legal identity and is fundamental to securing other rights. However, people born in forced migration contexts may be denied this right for practical or socio-legal reasons (Cowper-Smith and Kane, 2024). As shown in Chapter 1, most refugees and displaced people are hosted in countries of the

Global South, which sometimes lack capacity to register births, even for their own citizens. Birth registration fees are a barrier for some families. Children born in transit, on dangerous journeys, to undocumented or unmarried parents, and/or in remote areas may also not be registered for logistical, security, or legal reasons. States may also deny birth registration due to socio-legal and gender discrimination. Some countries only allow fathers to register births, do not recognize children from same-sex relationships, and/or require marriage certificates (UNHCR & UNICEF, 2021). For example, many Syrian refugee children born in Jordan are not registered at birth because the Jordanian state does not recognize traditional Islamic marriage, which is common among Syrian refugees (Shanneik, 2021). As a result, these refugees cannot register the births of their children, who are deemed to be born out of wedlock (IHRC, 2015).

The significant number of people in migration contexts who do not have birth certificates has led to a phenomenon of "bureaucratic birthdates" (Seibel, 2016a), where international organizations arbitrarily assign a January 1 or July 1 birthdate with a year approximated by memories of significant political, historical, social, or natural events. While this allows refugees to access services, it can create problems when birth years are off significantly. For example, in my refugee sponsorship experience in Canada, I encountered an Afghan child who had lost a year of formal schooling due to displacement and was then placed two grades ahead of where they should have been due to a birthdate error in their paperwork. In addition to the challenges of adapting to a new school environment in a new language, this child effectively "skipped" three grades, which posed significant learning challenges. The private sponsorship of refugees (PSR) program in Canada—through which the Alkarnake family also arrived—highlights differential expectations of childhood across different places. In the Canadian context, chronological age is the basis for legally binding rules that determine when a person can drive, marry, engage in consensual sexual relationships, etc. Throughout my many experiences as a sponsor over 15 years, I have also seen how Canadian-based sponsors may try to impose what they believe to be normatively superior or culturally appropriate beliefs about what children should and should not do. Because of the unequal dependency relationship baked into the PSR program, differential socially constructed views about childhood and parenting pose ethical dilemmas.

Children born outside of their parents' country of citizenship are also at greater risk of statelessness. A stateless person is "not considered a national by any State under the operation of its law" (Article 1(1), 1954 Convention relating to the Status of Stateless Persons). Under the CRC, states are legally obliged to grant citizenship to children who are born in their territory if they are not recognized as citizens of another country. However, in practice, this does not always occur. For example, children born to Rohingya refugees in Bangladesh are denied citizenship by the Myanmar government (as are their parents), but are also not granted Bangladeshi citizenship (Milton *et al.*, 2017).

When children do gain citizenship in their country of birth, they may have a different nationality than their parents and siblings, as Eyad's experience shows in the example above. In some cases, this causes family separation across borders. For example, the children of a married couple from Nigeria and the Philippines were born in Nigeria, the Philippines, and the US. When their asylum claim in Canada was unsuccessful, the father was deported to Nigeria, while the children and their mother faced deportation to the Philippines until UN Human Rights Committee intervened (Stevenson and Rukavina, 2023).

Early years in displacement contexts

The early years of a person's life are a period of rapid physical, cognitive, social, and emotional development. Displacement can have a significant impact on these aspects of development (Stevens, Siraj, and Kong, 2023). One challenge that families of infants and young children face is access to adequate, nutritional, and culturally appropriate food. In countries of first asylum in the Global South, limited funding and inadequate food rations can cause starvation, dehydration, and severe malnutrition, limiting growth and development of infants and young children (Khuri *et al.*, 2022). Those arriving in the Global North as refugee claimants or resettled refugees are at less risk of starvation, but still face food insecurity and limited access to, and knowledge of, available nutritious food sources, increasing the risk of diet-related disease (Nur *et al.*, 2021).

Young children in displacement contexts often have limited access to culturally appropriate, affordable early childhood education and care (ECEC). Lamb's (2020, p. 129) research in Australia, for example, found "most refugee families did not participate in quality ECEC, with key areas of exclusion being poverty, language, ethno-cultural discrimination, cultural divergence and trauma.

Non-enrolment of children was indicative of systemic barriers, such as prohibitive fees". Similarly, Bove and Sharmahd (2020) show that in many European countries refugee and asylum-seeking children are "invisible" in ECEC programming, and when they do access these services, they tend to be of poorer quality and/or not culturally appropriate. To address these systemic barriers, researchers in Canada have called for bridging programs that attend to the specific linguistic, cultural, religious, and financial realities of children and families from displacement backgrounds (Poureslami *et al.*, 2013). Similarly, Lamb (2020, p. 129) argues, "Refugee families require services that foster culturally safe and secure environments; promote language rights; and implement trauma-informed, anti-discriminatory, culturally sustaining pedagogies."

ECEC programs not only have a positive impact on young children's cognitive, social, and emotional development, but also on their families. Research in Germany shows that the families of children who accessed ECEC services also had better settlement and integration outcomes (Gambaro, Neidhöfer, and Spiess, 2021). In this study, parents benefited from social connections and linguistic and cultural contacts made through their children's ECEC participation. Having children in care also freed up parents, especially mothers, to enter the labor force (Gambaro, Neidhöfer, and Spiess, 2021). Thinking about children within household, family, and community relationships also opens up understandings of intra- and intergenerational aspects of forced migration experiences, as will be explored further in Chapter 6.

The social construction of childhood in forced migration contexts

As explained in the introduction, different stages of the life course, including childhood, are socially constructed. This means that people experience childhood differently depending on their social location within families, communities, and intersecting power structures and identities like gender, sexual orientation, disability, religion, race, ethnicity, and class. Childhood also varies across time and place. In the example above, Eyad's childhood in Canada in the second and third decades of the twenty-first century will be very different than what his parents experienced growing up in Syria in the late twentieth century.

Contexts of displacement add another layer to the social construction of childhood as children of immigrants and refugees straddle at least two cultures, even if they were born in the host country. There are many studies on children's experiences in "hyphenated identities" (Song, 2010; Behtoui, 2021) across different cultural or national belongings, such as "Haitian-Canadian" or "Muslim-American". Others describe the multi-faceted identities of first-generation children (Oberoi, 2016) who migrate with their families (like Eyad's brothers in the example above) or second-generation children who are born in a host country to immigrant parents (Portes and MacLeod, 1996; Hirsch, 2019)— like Eyad. Some researchers refer to the first-generation children and young people as the 1.5 generation, to highlight their hybrid identities—not as familiar with their country of origin as their parents, but not as integrated into the host country as children born there (Vaquera, Castañeda, and Aranda, 2022). Indeed, communities who have experienced prolonged displacement may include children who were born in exile, and then resettled to a third country (like Eyad's sister). While this research is varied and extensive, the key points of convergence are that children who experience childhood in more than one culture can code switch—literally and metaphorically (White, 2012)—and adapt their behavior to different circumstances, but can also feel like they do not belong anywhere (Guo, Maitra, and Guo, 2019). They also navigate different cultural and social expectations of childhood and what is considered to be appropriate behavior, upbringing, roles and responsibilities of children.

Participation in formal education is a significant way in which children and young people are socialized into the host country's culture, norms, and national identity. It is also often a key motivation in family's migration decisions. For example, in the story above, Ibtesam Alkarnake said, "I sacrificed for the family. I felt like the other decision was to postpone arrival into Canada and that's going to hurt my kids for school and their life in Canada" (cited in Thurton, 2017). Formal education also provides immersion in the host country's language (Stolk, Kaplan, and Szwarc, 2023) and culture. This means that children often acquire advanced language skills much more quickly than adults. They are linguistically and socially able to translate and interpret for their parents and other adult family and community members (Morales, Yakushko, and Castro, 2012; Hynie, Guruge, and Shakya, 2013; Bauer, 2016). These important "brokering" and interpretation roles provide them with a way to contribute and influence their family's integration. However, they also take time and energy away from studying and socializing and may lead to the "adultification" of refugee and migrant children's middle and late childhood. Such situations can also contribute to intergenerational tension, as will be discussed in Chapter 6.

Adolescence and youth

While the CRC defines a child as under the age of 18, in many displacement contexts, older children take on adult-like roles at an earlier age. Some of these transitions will be explained in more detail in the next chapter. Here, it is worthwhile noting that many cultures and religions mark rites of passage at or around puberty, with significant social age implications (see Chapter 1). As a result, while young people under the chronological age of 18 may be treated as children for legal, policy, and programming purposes, adolescents often take on some socially significant adult-like roles and responsibilities in displacement contexts (Sleijpen *et al.*, 2016).

Much of the literature and policy for refugee children focuses on early and middle childhood, but being displaced in adolescence brings different experiences than for younger children (Maguire, 2012). First, formal education is much more challenging. Unlike universal access to primary school, secondary school is not always mandatory nor free, especially in countries of first asylum in the Global South (Dryden-Peterson, 2016). In the context of limited financial and employment opportunities in the Global North, once older children are no longer legally required to attend school, they may drop out to support themselves or their families through childcare, domestic work, and/or remunerated employment (Moinolnolki and Han, 2017). Language barriers for displaced children in middle and secondary school may be more significant than in younger grades because the material is more difficult and because native-born children have greater literacy skills at higher levels of schooling (Stolk, Kaplan, and Szwarc, 2023). Many school boards in countries of the Global North place students in grades that are commensurate with their chronological age, posing particular challenges for students who have had little to no previous formal education, or whose education has been interrupted due to displacement (Antony-Newman and Niyozov, 2023). As the material gets difficult, it is more challenging to "catch up", resulting in poor learning outcomes, dropouts, and/or streaming into technical trades (Nichols, Ha, and Tyyskä, 2019).

Second, older children who have passed puberty also have specific needs related to culturally appropriate and gender-affirming sexual and reproductive healthcare (Maheen *et al.*, 2021). They may also face conflicting or diverging views about what is appropriate sexual behavior between their home and host cultures (Secor-Turner *et al.*, 2021). In some cases, parents may refuse consent for their children to attend information sessions on reproductive health, sexuality, sexual orientation, and gender identity (Morrison-Beedy *et al.*, 2022). Young refugees and asylum seekers who identify as part of the LGBTQI+ community face particular challenges in accessing appropriate reproductive health and mental health services (Morales *et al.*, 2022).

Third, as alluded to above, older children are legally entitled to engage in remunerated employment. This work is often a financial necessity for themselves and their family and can sometimes contribute to skills development and upward mobility. However, precarious, low-paid survival work also interferes with schooling, socializing, and class-based mobility (Febria and Jones, 2023).

Fourth, adolescents have particular mental health needs. While all children, particularly those who have experienced violence and war, need mental health supports (Hodes and Vostanis, 2019), adolescence is also a time of hormonal change. These normal developmental issues are overlaid with the stress and strain and dual identity issues of displacement (d'Abreu, Castro-Olivo, and Ura, 2019; Noori, 2020). Moreover, older children are more likely to be cognitively and emotionally aware of the real financial, physical, and emotional stresses that their parents, caregivers, siblings, and families are experiencing, and may also have increased responsibilities in their households, families, and communities, resulting in additional pressures on their own mental health.

Unaccompanied minors and separated children

While much of this chapter has focused on children within family and community relationships, it is important to note that some children and young people cross borders alone, or are separated from their families due to state policies and laws. Policymakers and practitioners may distinguish between separated children and unaccompanied minors. They designate as "separated children" those who migrate without a parent or legal guardian, but who travel with an adult who is responsible—formally or informally—for their care. In contrast, "unaccompanied minors" is a more specialized category of children under the age of 18 who are "separated from both parents and other relatives and are not being cared for by an adult who, by law or custom, is responsible for doing so" (ICRC, 2004, n.p.). Some researchers prefer the term "independent child migration" to acknowledge the agency of children and young people migrating alone (Orgocka and Clark-Kazak, 2012). Indeed, in some cases, family separation is part of a deliberate individual or collective strategy to escape intergenerational violence, or to manage risks across household and family members.

While accurate statistics are difficult to obtain, indications are that the number of separated and unaccompanied children has increased in recent years. For example, in fiscal year 2022, US immigration officials encountered a record 152,000 unaccompanied minors at or near the US-Mexico border (Cheatham and Roy, 2023). EU member states received 39,520 first-time applications for protection from unaccompanied minors in 2022— a 45% increase compared to 2021 (Euro-Med Human Rights Monitor, 2023).

In addition to benefiting from the general rights under the CRC, unaccompanied minors and separated children are entitled to specific protections. Article 20 provides for "special protection and assistance provided by the state" for any child "temporarily or permanently deprived of his or her family environment" (CRC 1990, article 20, para. 1). UNHCR maintains that unaccompanied minors should be appointed a guardian as soon as possible (UNHCR, 1997). In some jurisdictions, like Canada, they are also appointed a designated representative to help them navigate the refugee determination process (Immigration and Refugee Board Canada, 2023). However, in reality, it may be difficult for unaccompanied minors to exercise their rights. Children who have navigated difficult journeys alone are resourceful and knowledgeable, sometimes clashing with socially constructed notions of innocence and immaturity typically associated with children and young people in liberal western democracies (McLaughlin, 2017). This has led some states, such as the United Kingdom and Spain (Vives, 2020), to suspect the veracity of their claims to both childhood and asylum (Clark-Kazak, forthcoming) and rely heavily on problematic age assessments to root out "imposter children" (Silverman, 2016).

Family separation has also been used as a deliberate policy of some states to try to deter migration. For example, under the Trump administration between 2017 to 2021, the US government separated at least 3,900 children, some as young as a few months old, from their parents as part of a "zero-tolerance" policy to try to deter irregular migration along the US-Mexico border (Halpert, 2023). Jose Luis Martinez, an asylum seeker from Honduras who was separated from his three daughters aged 10, 12, and 14 at the Texas border in 2018, still remembers when US border officials took his children away: ""They were crying and crying", he said. "Their mother had already died. All they wanted was their daddy. I was the only thing they had" (cited in Halpert, 2023). Mr. Martinez had to wait four years to be reunited with his daughters. As at March 2023, almost 1,000 children were still awaiting reunification (Halpert, 2023).

Conclusion

This chapter has analyzed some of the key issues relating to birth and childhood in contexts of forced displacement. While child rights are theoretically universal, in reality, where a child is born and grows up has significant implications for their ability to exercise their rights, including the right to birth registration, nationality, education, health, and family unity. Children and young people in displacement contexts straddle multiple cultural and social contexts, resulting in hybrid—and at times competing—views about socially appropriate behavior, roles, and responsibilities. The liminality of transitioning to adulthood across borders will be explored in more detail in the next chapter.

3
Displaced young people's liminality in time, space, and place

Introduction: Betwixt and between

The period of youth is often a time marked with transitions from childhood to adulthood through post-secondary education, full-time employment, marriage, and/or becoming a parent. In migration contexts, these transitions are layered onto uncertain and dynamic migration decisions, relationships, and policies. Liminality describes an ambiguous state between phases. Many young people in migration situations face a double liminality as both their migration status and life course transitions are "on pause" for long periods of time (Gonzales, 2016). After they turn 18, they no longer benefit from legal protections accorded to children under international law, but they do not yet fully benefit from access to adult opportunities.

It should be noted that there is no internationally recognized definition of "young people" or "youth". The United Nations and its associated agencies, like UNICEF and UNESCO, define "youth" as "persons between the age of 15 and 24 years", in accordance with a 1981 UN general assembly resolution (UN General Assembly, 1981). However, as noted in Chapters 1 and 2, chronological age is problematic in migration contexts. Therefore, in this chapter, I use the terms "young people", "youth", and "young adults" to describe the circumstances of people who are in transitional stages between childhood and adulthood. In some cases, migration causes a prolongation of these transitional stages because of uncertainties surrounding migration status or citizenship (Clark-Kazak, 2011; Grabska, Regt, and Franco, 2018). In other cases, this transition is expedited through early marriage, employment, and/or adultification, where children and young people are treated as adults (Puig, 2002).

We will now turn to the example of undocumented young people in the United States to demonstrate how migration status impacts key life course transitions. As Gonzalez et al. (2018, p. 345) argue, "In the United States at the start of the 21st century, coming of age constitutes a socially stratified life course process, unequally distributed among young people according to differences in class, race, and immigration status." The experiences of undocumented young people in the US show how precarious immigration status can prolong the liminality of youth by postponing or prohibiting adult transitions like higher education, employment, and marriage. At the same time, young people may face adult responsibilities—including for older relatives—even as they are prevented from obtaining full adult social status.

Sadhana's story: Undocumented young people in the United States

For undocumented immigrant youth—those who arrive to the United States at early ages and lack formal legal immigration status—the dawning of adolescence has been likened to a waking nightmare (Gonzales & Chavez, 2012), wherein youth begin to directly encounter legal barriers associated with their undocumented status and come to terms with how these transitions will affect their future prospects. (Gonzales *et al.*, 2018, p. 346)

The US has the largest undocumented population in the world, with over 11 million people estimated to be "unauthorized" in 2019 (Migration Policy Institute, 2019). In 2012, then President Obama launched the Deferred Action for Childhood Arrivals (DACA) program to allow eligible young people who entered the US irregularly as children to apply for a driver's license, social security number, and work permit. While DACA did not give these young people official legal status or US citizenship, it did remove some of the key barriers to transitions to adulthood, namely independent, regularized livelihoods. In 2017, President Trump announced a phasing out of DACA, which triggered a series of court cases, but restrictions to DACA were still implemented. In 2021, President Biden issued an executive order to reinstate DACA, but legal challenges have prevented this from happening.

In the end, 817,911 people were approved for DACA from 2012 to 2020 (Congressional Research Service, 2021). Many more were never eligible and remain undocumented or in precarious immigration status. However, the existence of DACA provided a "natural experiment"[3] to observe some of the positive changes to adult transitions that occurred where certain immigration-related barriers were removed (Gonzales *et al.*, 2018). For example, in the car-centric context of the US, a driver's license is a rite of passage (Gonzales *et al.*, 2018), but also a necessity for some jobs. It also serves as a piece of identification to prove chronological age and to open bank accounts. For some DACA participants, the ability to work legally also increased their access to training and educational opportunities (Gonzales *et al.*, 2018, p. 351). Others benefited from health insurance provided by formal employment. DACA provides important insights into how immigration status affects key life course events in young people's lives.

For example, Sadhana and her family overstayed their tourist visas when she was 13 years old. She asked people to call her "Ashley" and believed her lack of status was a "stigma": "I was afraid to come out to my friends. I thought they would see me as inferior and treat me differently" (*My Lives of Uncertainty: Sadhana Singh at TEDxWilliam&Mary*, 2018). She helped her parents navigate the US system, but she faced barriers to participating in adolescent life, such as getting a driver's license. She didn't have much of a social life because she didn't have an ID and couldn't drive. "When everyone wanted to know what colleges her impeccable grades had earned her admission to, she said she was still waiting to hear back" (Contrera, 2019). This situation had an impact on Sadhana's mental health and social development: "I was completely in the shadows. I was never able to go to a counsellor or teacher and explain my situation. I was alienated. I was alone. But life went on" (*My Lives of Uncertainty: Sadhana Singh at TEDxWilliam&Mary*, 2018).

At age 19, Sadhana took a job to help out her parents (Friends Committee on National Legislation, n.d.). "For nine years after high school, Sadhana languished, living at home, working as a lab technician for an archaeology company and sinking into a depression she struggled to explain" (Contrera, 2019). Sadhana recalls, "Home and work was all I had … I would roam around the house in a daze as if I were a ghost with unfinished business" (*My Lives of Uncertainty: Sadhana Singh at TEDxWilliam&Mary*, 2018). Even after DACA was announced, Sadhana could not afford to go to college because undocumented students do not have access to federal loans and she had to pay out-of-state tuition and her family couldn't afford it. "I had to wait for close to a decade for my chance. It was difficult to watch my friends move on with their lives while I was stuck in the same place. In my early twenties I was languishing. I felt repressed, suffocated, left behind. I was going nowhere year, after year, after year" (*My Lives of Uncertainty: Sadhana Singh at TEDxWilliam&Mary*, 2018).

However, she finally won a Dream.US scholarship to study at Trinity Washington University. "This scholarship was my ticket to my next life" (*My Lives of Uncertainty: Sadhana Singh at TEDxWilliam&Mary*, 2018). At the time, she reflected, "my confidence has skyrocketed at Trinity being surrounded by so much support. I've always been outspoken, I just never had the agency before" (Friends Committee on National Legislation, n.d.). But, she still worried about the future: "I don't want to have to keep renewing my life every 2 years. America has been my home for over 2 decades but for most of that time I couldn't take part in it" (*My Lives of Uncertainty: Sadhana Singh at TEDxWilliam&Mary*, 2018). She was anxious about how to move forward after university: "I need to know that I can live my life without uncertainty and fear at every moment. I need to know that I can make plans without worrying about whether I or my loved one will be detained and deported. … I need to know that the country will see me as a human being, not as an invading alien" (*My Lives of Uncertainty: Sadhana Singh at TEDxWilliam&Mary*, 2018).

She met and fell in love with another undocumented migrant, My Ford. They wanted to have children, but they did not want their children to suffer the same fate as them. Eventually, the couple obtained visas to work in Canada, with the possibility of permanent residence. But leaving the US meant that they would not be able to return for 10 years (Contrera, 2019). And, as undocumented migrants, her parents would never be able to visit her in Canada.

"She stood between her husband and her father, her future and her past. The next morning, My Ford would drive the U-Haul north to a four-bedroom house he had rented for them in Ontario. Her father would board a bus and leave for Georgia. Sadhana would be alone in Virginia, trying to gather the strength to follow through on the plan: Take a flight to Toronto. Show her new visa. Leave behind the country her parents had hoped would give her a better life, so she could give the same to her own children one day" (Contrera, 2019).

Post-secondary education

As shown in Sadhana's story, post-secondary education and training opportunities are a key aspect of many young people's lives, as well as an important source of social capital for their future. Young people may view education as a way of "becoming somebody" (Crivello, 2009) or as a means of social mobility (Clark-Kazak, 2011; 2012). However, while primary and secondary education is free in many host contexts, post-secondary education is often prohibitively expensive. As experienced by Sadhana, young people without permanent migration status, including refugees, asylum seekers and undocumented migrants, often face high international student fees, and are not always eligible for loans and scholarships that are available to domestic students.

On the other hand, in some cases, postsecondary education opportunities cause migration—either internally or across borders. For example, the World University Services of Canada has a Student Refugee Program, which resettles young people aged 18 to 25 to Canada through peer sponsorship at over 100 campuses (McKee et al., 2019). Complementary education pathways have been identified as a way to address prolonged displacement and its disproportionate effect on young people by using postsecondary education opportunities as a way to expand protection (UNHCR, n.d.). A Global Task force on Third Country Education Pathways was also established. Despite these initiatives, access to post-secondary education is limited for young people in forced migration contexts, with UNHCR estimating that only 7% of refugees had access to higher education in 2023 (UNHCR, n.d.).

Even when they do access postsecondary learning, young people with lived experience of forced migration may face structural barriers to academic success, retention, and completion. Many students with displaced backgrounds must work—sometimes full-time—while completing their studies. They may also have gendered caregiving and interpretation responsibilities in intergenerational families (Shakya et al., 2014). Students may not know how to access counselling and academic support services (Stermac et al., 2012) and are often ineligible for government-funded settlement services. Racialized and visibly religious students face additional layers of discrimination due to racism, xenophobia, and/or Islamophobia (Bajwa et al., 2018). Newcomer LGBTQI+ students also report homophobia, transphobia, and gendered discrimination (Marshall, 2021). Some, like Sadhana, feel like they are constantly navigating between different lives. As a key to social mobility and integration, but also transition to adulthood, postsecondary education is thus an important life course transition shaped by migration.

Full-time employment

Employment is also an important milestone in the transition from youth to adulthood as the degree of financial security may affect life course decisions, like marriage and parenthood (Gonzales, 2016). Work experience may also be integral to young people's sense of independence and a stepping stone for future employment (Perreira, Harris, and Lee 2007). However, young people from forced migration backgrounds may face structural barriers in the labor market, including non-recognition of credentials and experience (Guo, 2009; Lee et al., 2020; Banerjee, 2022), limited social capital (Lamba, 2008), precarious migration status (Jackson and Bauder, 2014), institutionalized racism (Creese and Wiebe, 2012), and/or anti-immigrant bias in hiring practices (Banerjee, Reitz, and Oreopoulos, 2018). Undocumented young people and others without work permits face legal barriers to meaningful, stable employment (Gonzales, 2016). As a result, they may end up in precarious, low-paid employment, sometimes under the table. Perreira et al.'s (2007, p. 8) research shows "patterns of spatial isolation, discrimination, and labor-market bifurcation between high- and low-skilled jobs can affect their orientations to school and access to jobs". The lack of dignified work has implications for mental health, as shown in Sadhana's story.

Similarly, pressure to support their family financially can hinder academic achievement (Perreira, Harris, and Lee, 2007, p. 6) and, by extension, access to higher paid and secure employment. As Gonzalez et al. (2018, p. 348) argue, "family need keeps them lingering in adolescence". The financial dependence of parents and other older relatives jeopardizes young people's ability to provide for their own future. Ironically, it also keeps them in a child-like social age limbo where they are not yet considered to be full adults. As Gonzales (2016, p. xxi) explains, "They are hostages to time. While their dreams are on hold, they must manage the pressures of finding employment, paying the bills, and supporting family members."

Marriage

In many cultures, marriage culturally symbolizes initiation into adulthood. It also changes familial and intergenerational relationships. Marriage interacts with migration in many ways. First, it can be a cause of migration (Bélanger and Haemmerli, 2019; Charsley *et al.*, 2020; Gardner, 2021). Spouses are one of the largest categories of migrant settlement (Charsley *et al.*, 2020). In some cases, children and young people are forced into transnational marriages either through family pressure (Zeweri, 2024) or trafficking (Quek, 2018). There have also been cases of people—mainly women and girls—fleeing forced marriages and/or claiming refugee status on the basis of gender-based persecution relating to marriage practices (Dauvergne and Millbank, 2011).

Second, forced migration changes the nature of marriage. In some contexts, children and young people are pressured into early and underage marriages in the context of limited choices for themselves and their families (Cherri *et al.*, 2017; Elnakib *et al.*, 2021; Islam, Khan, and Rahman, 2021). In other cases, forced migration causes delays in marriage as young people wait for secure immigration status and/or employment before marrying (Clark-Kazak, 2011). Marriage practices and ceremonies may also change in the context of inter-cultural and inter-religious marriages, or due to adaptation to host community norms and/or socioeconomic conditions in forced migration contexts.

Third, in some cases marital status changes because of movement across international borders. Cohabitation, common-law, and same-sex marriages are recognized in some countries and not in others (Dunton, 2012; Gaucher, 2018). Similarly, polygamous marriages are illegal in some contexts, so some spouses are not recognized as family members for resettlement and sponsorship purposes (Neikirk, 2018). Irregular migration status can also pose barriers to forming relationships and to marriage recognition and registration, as some DACA experiences show

(Gonzales, 2016; Carcamo, 2019). For example, Carcamo (2019) cites the case of a 23-year-old DACA recipient "whose legal status keeps him from dating seriously. He makes sure not to get too attached because of a feeling in his gut that, one day, he will be deported. And he won't date another DACA recipient or person without legal status."

Fourth, borders can interrupt the social meanings and relationships ascribed to marriage (Carver, 2021). Traditional cultural practices may be difficult to replicate in new resettlement contexts, especially for religious minorities (Tonui and Mitschke, 2022). Family members may not be able to attend marriage ceremonies in other countries because of visa requirements, financial barriers, and physical limitations (Halabi, 2023). This means that young people in forced migration contexts may experience one of the most socially significant aspects of their lives and transition to adulthood—marriage—without the support or presence of key family members and traditions.

Parenthood

Becoming a parent is a life course milestone that also impacts social age and intergenerational relationships, as the birth of a child also creates a new generation. In Chapter 2, I discussed birth from the perspective of the infant's status and citizenship. Migration also has a significant impact on parents, particularly in relation to timing of births (Wolf, 2016; Yoshida and Amoyaw, 2020). Indeed, as Sadhana's story shows, young people may choose to migrate to provide better opportunities for their (unborn) children. However, as in Sadhana's case, this migration may mean that they raise their children without familial support, as grandparents and other family members are unable to cross borders.

Others wait until they have legal status. As one DACA recipient recounted (Carcamo, 2019), "I feel that I wouldn't be able to live with myself if I were to have a child and I were, for some reason, to get kicked out of this country and not be able to come back." Indeed, migration, detention, and deportation can cause family separation. In these cases, young people may take on parental roles of their younger siblings, as will be discussed in Chapter 6.

Conclusion

Youth and migration are particularly intense periods of future projection, of unsettled identifications with the past and of cautious or bold but always high-stakes experimentations in the present. (Bialas, 2023, p. 126)

This chapter shows how "coming of age" through significant life course events like attending postsecondary education, finding full-time employment, marrying and/or having children, map on to migration experiences. Young people in forced migration contexts also live "betwixt and between" different places. Borders may separate them from their immediate and extended family, complicating or prohibiting familial participation in life course events, like marriage and parenting. They also navigate different cultural and societal expectations in relation to transitions to adulthood. Migration status has real consequences for life course decisions and experiences.

In some cases, young migrants experience "double waithood" (Van Raemdonck, 2023) as they wait for both adulthood and permanent status. As one young undocumented young person told Gonzales (2016, p. 3), "I've missed out on so much time. While my friends have been busy building their careers with internships and entry-level jobs that have given them real experience, on the job, I've got to start from scratch." At other times, youth is truncated or accelerated as young people are pressured into early marriage, work, and parenthood in the context of limited choices. I will return to theme of time at the end of the book. The next chapter shows how the adult-centric approach to migration ignores other aspects of the life course.

4
Adulthood as default "refugeeness": The limitations of an adult-centric approach to forced migration

International and national laws and policies often explicitly or implicitly conceptualize forced displacement as an adult condition, which is also gendered (Clark-Kazak, 2025). How does this adult-centricity limit policies, programming, and understandings of forced migration? This chapter explores the adult norm of "refugeeness" juxtaposed against the lived realities across the life course. It also shows how "vulnerable" categories both reinforce and challenge problematic adult-centricity. In other words, categories of exception reify the adult-centric norm, at the same time as they expose the large number of people—indeed, the majority—who fall outside that norm. We turn now to an example of Afghan refugees in the United Kingdom to illustrate and problematize adult-centric approaches to forced migration.

Zahra's experience as an Afghan refugee in the UK

In August 2021, Zahra Joya fled Afghanistan to London, United Kingdom (UK) with her three sisters and her 15-year-old brother. As a well-known journalist documenting women's rights through her news agency, Rukhshana Media, Zahra was at risk of persecution (Kelly, 2024).

Zahra and her four younger siblings were on one of the last evacuation flights out of Kabul after the Taliban took power. They left their parents and two older siblings behind, where they were threatened by the Taliban and fled to Pakistan. Once the Pakistani government started sending Afghans back to Afghanistan, Zahra's parents applied for a visa to the UK, but the application was denied. As Zahra says, "It is very painful that I could not find a safe place for my family in this vast world. This feeling is devastating and hopeless. I fear I'll never see them again and I feel responsible as I know that my journalism has a part to play in their situation" (cited in Kelly, 2024).

Zahra has refugee status in the UK, where she continues her work with Rukhshana Media (Amanpour, 2023). Her sisters attend university. However, her teenage brother has not adapted as well to life in the UK. Zahra is concerned about him: "It is especially sad for my little brother, who has been separated from my mother and has suffered a lot. He is losing weight and is struggling and

I am not his mother. I do what I can but I can't give him what he needs" (Kelly, 2024).

Zahra's story highlights three key points explored in this chapter. First, the individualistic approach to determining migration status is aged and gendered. Second, the adult-centricity of much forced migration law, programming, and policy results in gaps for people in other stages of the life course. Third, the category approach to "vulnerables" both constructs certain age groups as categories of exception, but also includes a majority of people in forced migration contexts, thereby undermining the administrative and normative utility of the concept.

Individualistic approach to definitions of displacement and refugee status determination

As discussed in Chapter 1, the UN 1951 Refugee Convention lays the foundation for international legal definition of a "refugee" and informs refugee status determination in many Global North countries. The refugee definition is individualistic in that it defines "a refugee" in the singular who, "owing to well-founded fear of being persecuted for reasons of race, religion, nationality, membership of a particular social group or political opinion, is outside the country of [their] nationality and is unable or, owing to such fear, is unwilling to avail [themself] of the protection of that country". While group-based *prima facie* recognition does occur, particularly in Africa (Durieux, 2008), most liberal democracies in the Global North assess individual claims against the Convention definition, with some variations in national laws and processes (Costello, Nalule, and Ozkul, 2020).

In the UK, this means that only the applicant receives refugee status. While dependents, such as spouses and children, can usually stay in the UK for as long as the applicant, they have to make their own asylum claim if they wish to also have refugee status (Madziva, 2016; Government of the United Kingdom, n.d.). So, in the example above, Zahra and each of her siblings, including her 15-year-old brother, must apply separately for refugee status. While Zahra's siblings are indirectly at risk of persecution from the Taliban because of her journalism (as demonstrated by threats against her parents and siblings who remained in Afghanistan), they would have to convince the UK authorities of their individual right to asylum.

The UN refugee definition is technically "age-neutral, applying to all individual irrespective of age" (Pobjoy, 2017). It should also be noted that the *travaux préparatoires*[4] recognized the specific needs of children, especially unaccompanied minors (Pobjoy, 2017). However, in reality, this supposed age-neutrality often translates into adult-centric processes that ignore the specific rights and needs of people across the life course. For example, as mentioned in Chapter 2, unaccompanied minors are appointed a designated representative to help them navigate the refugee status determination processes in some countries. Similarly, older people are sometimes listed as part of vulnerable groups who can request accommodations during the refugee determination process (Clark-Kazak, 2025). While these age-sensitive exceptions expand equitable access to refugee status determination, they also expose the underlying ageism of such systems that render these accommodations necessary.

Indeed, research across many jurisdictions indicate that most refugee status determination processes do not uphold the best interests of the child principle for several reasons (Bhabha, 2004; Lundberg, 2011; Smyth, 2014; Ghebrai and Ballucci, 2022; Rap, 2022; Ciufo, forthcoming). First, in many cases, children's views and experiences are not adequately solicited and taken into account in asylum decisions (Smyth, 2014; Rap, 2022). As Rap (2022) argues, "Refugee children are often neither recognised as rights holders nor as active agents in asylum procedures." Second, children are not given sufficient information on the refugee determination process in a format and language they can under-stand (Rap, 2022; Ciufo, forthcoming). Third, decision-makers do not adequately assess the impact of asylum outcomes on chil-dren (Lundberg, 2011; Ghebrai and Ballucci, 2022). Lundberg (2011) contends that "children's rights are treated as secondary to the national interest of keeping overall migration numbers down". The outcome is particularly egregious in cases where chil-dren are citizens by birth, but whose parents are deemed not to be refugees, and are thus subject to detention and deportation (Bhabha, 2009).

Similarly, while technically gender-neutral, the refugee definition is interpreted through gendered refugee determination pro-cesses. The 1951 definition was conceived in the context of post-World War II, where political dissidents were often perceived to be male (Aberman, 2014). However, as Aberman (forthcoming) shows, "As 'refugeeness' became increasingly depoliticized, it also became feminized." This feminization led to notions of vulnerabil-ity and passivity in the gendered construction of the "ideal refu-gee" (Fiddian-Qasmiyeh, 2014). Feminization and infanticization intersected in the "women-and-children" constructs "aggregated as one disadvantaged and neglected group" (Bhabha, 2004). There has also been a tendency to collapse diversity of experience within a "vulnerability" framework, as will be discussed further below.

On a more positive note, some countries now recognize gender, gender identity, and sexual orientation as grounds for persecution as part of a "particular social group". In relation to the Afghan example above,

> The European Union Agency for Asylum (EUAA) has concluded that the measures introduced by the Taliban affect the rights and freedoms of women and girls, put them, in general, at risk of persecution and make them eligible for refugee status. While EUAA guidance is not legally binding, in accordance with the EUAA Regulation (Article 11(3)), EU Member States are required to consider it when evaluating asylum claims. (Leclerc and Shreeves, 2023)

Despite being gender-progressive, such approaches still foreground the individual in the refugee determination process. Such individualistic approaches to refugee status determination overlook the fact that refugees are connected to others in kinship, community, and religious networks.

Notion of dependence and sponsorship

When refugee claimants and resettled refugees are recognized as being members of families, there are ageist and gendered assumptions, particularly in the framing of dependency and sponsorship. As shown in the UK example above, children and spouses are usually listed as dependents, and sometimes have a different immigration status than the principal applicant. Underlying the "dependence" discourse are social age constructions of children as being financially and emotionally dependent on their parents. However, as shown in Chapters 2 and 3, children and young people play essential roles in their families through interpretation, domestic and child work, and remunerated employment. In other words, families are sites of mutually interdependent relationships, which are overlooked in the one-way interpretation of "dependence".

Policies on dependents not only overlook the important roles children and spouses play, but they also exacerbate gendered and ageist power relations by linking dependents' status to that of the principal applicant. Two nefarious results arise. First, if the principal applicant is deemed inadmissible or not a refugee, then their children and spouses also lose their right to remain in the country. Second, dependents can be trapped in abusive relationships because their immigration status is linked to their relationship with the principal applicant. For example, research by Hasager (2024) in Denmark found that "granting asylum to family-reunified women improves their economic integration, increases the probability of divorce and decreases their risk of being victims of violence".

Similarly, in refugee resettlement, UNHCR and receiving countries sometimes give priority to family reunification cases (Welfens and Bonjour 2021; see also next section). Because definitions of family vary (see Chapter 6), UNHCR (2023b) recommends that "family should be assessed on a case-by-case basis and informed by the principle of *dependency* and, in the case of children, Best Interests Procedures" (my emphasis). For example, the Government of Canada recognizes "de facto family members" (Immigration, 2018) in private refugee sponsorship to allow resettlement with a family of people outside of the immediate nuclear family who are deemed to depend—financially and socially—on the principal applicant (Clark-Kazak, 2025).

"Vulnerability" in refugee status determination and resettlement

As alluded to above, when age categories are mentioned in refugee determination and refugee settlement processes, they are often framed in terms of vulnerability. For example, the UK's Vulnerable Person Resettlement Scheme (VPRS) identifies "those in the greatest need, including people requiring urgent medical treatment, survivors of violence and torture, and women and children at risk" (UK Government, 2021). The last category frames vulnerability in gendered and ageist ways, echoing the "women-and-children" ideal refugee mentioned above.

UNHRC identifies seven priority resettlement submission categories: legal and/or physical protection needs; "women and girls at risk who are survivors, or are at risk, of gender-based violence"; "children and adolescents at risk, where resettlement has been assessed or determined to be in their best interests"; violence and/or torture survivors; medical needs; "restoring family unity"; and "lack of foreseeable alternative durable solutions" (UNHCR, 2023b, section 3.2). While three of the seven resettlement priorities relate to social age, there is no explicit mention of older people. This contrasts with the discursive frequency of references to older people in UNHCR's age, gender, and diversity policy (Clark-Kazak, 2009a).

The list is also notable because it includes both broad protection categories (for example, legal or medical) alongside categories of people (for example, "children and adolescents at risk"). This discursively dehumanizes people as categories (Clark-Kazak, 2009a; 2016). As I have argued elsewhere, this category approach to vulnerability is problematic for two key reasons (Clark, 2008). First, it essentializes certain age groups as inherently vulnerable, overlooking agency and intersecting power relations. Second, the expansive notion of vulnerability means that the majority of refugees in any given situation would be considered "vulnerable", thereby undermining the practical and administrative utility of the vulnerability assessment.

The vulnerability approach also reinforces the adult-centricity of refugee law, policy, and programming by positing "vulnerable" categories of exception ("women and children") against the norm of the adult male (Clark-Kazak, 2025). Vulnerability categorization thus overlooks the diverse, intersecting experiences of forced migration across the life course. It also creates policy and programming gaps. For example, Ukrainian displacement following the Russian invasion included a higher number of women, children, and older people than other contexts due to the demographic realities in Ukraine (see Chapter 5) and conscription of men aged 18 to 60. In this context, relatively large numbers of Ukrainian young people arrived alone in Canada, the

UK, and across the EU. Due to the adult-centricity of the response to Ukrainian displacement in these countries, there were widespread reports of children and young people being housed in inappropriate accommodation (Bora, 2022; Clark-Kazak, 2022), slipping through the cracks of children's aid societies (CWICE and JIAS, 2022) and, in some cases, disappearing or being trafficked (Townsend, 2023).

Conclusion

This chapter has demonstrated the individualistic, adult-centricity of the UN refugee definition and of asylum and resettlement processes in many liberal democracies in the Global North. Such an approach ignores the diversity of migration experiences and, consequently, leads to gaps in protection. Framing children and older people as inherently "vulnerable" and "dependent" overlooks the important roles they play in families but also, ironically, reinforces power inequities that constrain their agency. An equitable, rights-based approach requires a more nuanced understanding of social age and how it intersects with other power relations in determining different migration experiences.

5
Aging and dying in and out of place

Older people are often underrepresented in forced migration policy, programming, and research (Barbalet, 2018). They are more likely to remain behind—both voluntarily and involuntarily—in their country of origin. This chapter foregrounds the lived experiences of older people in contexts of (im)mobility and analyzes their changing social identities and relationships due to migration. It shows how older people experience displacement differently because of their social age and life course stage. This chapter also delves into cross-cultural and cross-border implications of significant life course events related to dying and death in exile.

It should be noted that conceptualizations of old age vary significantly across time and place, including through migration processes. As Dossa and Coe (2017, p. 7) argue, "Aging is a continuum and culturally it may even extend beyond our physical lives into the realm of ancestors and memory." In Global North neoliberal welfare states ordered by chronometric time, old age is often interpreted as the chronological age at which a person is eligible for state-funded pensions. Retirement age varies significantly across countries, as does the amount of the pension payment. In some cases, countries allow people to access pensions earlier, but at a lower rate. This linking of old age with state-funded benefits reinforces a notion of aging as posing a burden—to the state, families, and/or society. It also demonstrates the arbitrariness of any chronological age threshold as a definition of older persons. A social age approach highlights the social meanings ascribed to old age. In many contexts, "economic capital, life expectancy, and social roles … help determine life states, include when old age begins" (Dubus, 2018).

At an international level, the United Nations agencies often set 60 as the chronological age for defining older persons. However, UNHCR acknowledges the limitations of this approach, which implies homogeneity, overlooking the diversity of experiences of aging due to "factors such as disability; ethnic, religious or linguistic background; and sexual orientation, gender identity, gender expression and sex characteristics" (UNHCR, 2021, p. 5). Indeed, essentialist approaches to older people can be ageist, based in stereotypes rather than the lived realities of aging.

Unlike children, older people are not protected by specific international legal human rights instruments. While advocates have repeatedly called for a United Nations Convention on the rights of older persons, this is not yet a reality. In 1991, the UN General Assembly did adopt non-binding principles for older persons, which acknowledged existing universal rights and encouraged governments to adopt into domestic law and programs principles related to independence, participation, care, self-fulfillment, and dignity (UN General Assembly, 1991). In addition, UNHCR and HelpAge have developed guidelines for working with older persons in forced displacement (UNHCR, 2021). Despite these initiatives, older people still face ageism and barriers to accessing social services and human rights, as illustrated by the situation in Ukraine and discussed further in this chapter.

Stories of aging and displacement in and from Ukraine

Ukraine has been called the "oldest humanitarian crisis in the world" (AGE Platform Europe, n.d.) because of the large number of older people affected by conflict, violence, and displacement. Even before the Russian invasion, Ukraine was amongst the fastest aging countries in the world, with almost 17% of the population aged 65 or older in 2019 (UN Department of Economic and Social Affairs, 2019). The Russian attack disproportionately affected older Ukrainians for several reasons. First, the majority chose to stay in their homes or in Ukraine, making up a greater percentage of internally displaced who faced ongoing or threatened violence (Ducke and Riabenko, 2024; AGE Platform Europe, n.d.) in areas where humanitarian aid is harder to reach (HelpAge International, 2024b). For example, 81-year-old Liudmyla, said, "Where would I go? To a foreign country with a foreign language!? The travel itself would be very difficult for me, almost unrealistic. Come what may, I'm staying home" (HelpAge International, 2024a). Second, Ukrainians over the age 70 are more likely to live alone, with even more older people on their own after other family members fled or died and/or when conscription laws prevented men aged 18 to 59 from leaving Ukraine (HelpAge International, 2023b). Older Ukrainians who crossed international borders faced particular linguistic, physical, and social barriers to accessing services (HelpAge International, 2023a).

For example, some older Jewish Ukrainians, who fled Nazi persecution as children in World War II, have been relocated to neighboring countries through the Jewish Claims Conference, supported by other aid agencies (RetroReport, 2022). The largest number of Ukrainian refugees registered with UNHCR are in Germany, which has also set up specific programs for older refugees. Sonya Leibovna Tartakovskaya, an 83-year-old retired seamstress from Irpin, near Kyiv, who fled the Holocaust when she was three years old, now lives with other older Ukrainians in a retirement home in Berlin. "For 20 days, I was without gas, without water, without light … I lived alone, I have nobody. My whole family is long buried in cemeteries in different cities … But thanks to strangers, I got out of Irpin. My neighbors didn't leave me behind; they took me with them" (cited in Nicholson, 2022). This long period of isolation took its toll—while she normally weighs 100 pounds, when she arrived in Berlin, "I weighed almost half that" (cited in Nicholson, 2022). A recently arrived resident, 90-year-old Alla Ilyinichna Sinelnikova, says, "This war is a catastrophe. It's truly awful. I never thought I would live to see such horror for the second time in my life. I thought it was in my past, all over and done with. And now we're reliving it" (cited in Nicholson, 2022).

Limited research, policy and programming related to older people in forced migration

Forced migration studies has historically overlooked the specific experiences of older people who are displaced. As Bolzman (2014) points out, there is more research on aging after displacement, rather than the experiences of forced migration in old age. The lack of research with older people in forced migration can be partially explained by the relatively smaller number of older people who move across borders (Slade and Borovnik, 2018) and the bias in migration studies towards research on international movement, rather than internal displacement and immobility. As noted in the Ukrainian example, many older people did not leave their homes or did not cross an international border. However, this dearth of data also speaks to ageism and a lack of age-sensitivity in migration research, policy and practice (Kaga and Nakache, 2019).

Indeed, researchers have highlighted the "social invisibility of older men and women … in immigration policy" (Dossa and Coe, 2017, p. 3). Others have highlighted laws and policies that explicitly discriminate against older people on the basis of chronological age and/or their family status (Clark-Kazak, 2025). UNHCR recognizes this discrimination and the specific experiences of older people in its age, gender, and diversity mainstreaming policy (UNHCR, 2018). In their guidelines for working with older people in displacement contexts, UNHCR and HelpAge also acknowledge the intersectionality of old age with gender, sexual orientation, disability, and linguistic, ethnic, and/or religious discrimination that results in a diversity of experiences of aging in forced migration contexts (UNHCR, 2021).

Loneliness and mental health

Older people in contexts of displacement may face loneliness and mental health challenges related to feelings of "aging in the wrong place" (Hugman, Bartolomei, and Pittaway, 2004, p. 148).

For example, Horn and Fokkema (2023) found that almost half of survey respondents aged 45 and older who arrived in Germany as refugees between 2013 and 2016 "reported symptoms of loneliness. The major contributing factors included poor health, financial strain, lack of family ties in Germany, limited contact with Germans, insecure residence status, and perceived hostility towards them." Similarly, a study with older Somali refugees settled in Finland revealed mental health issues related to "both past traumatic war stress and present immigration-related stressors, including discrimination and racism" (Mölsä *et al.*, 2017). This research showed that family and religious networks helped to attenuate these mental health issues (Mölsä *et al.*, 2017). For older displaced people who do not have these social networks, the sense of loneliness, isolation, and loss of home is exacerbated (Bolzman, 2014; Slade and Borovnik, 2018). Indeed, a study with older Bhutanese refugees in the United States showed variable psychological adjustment to life in the US related to cultural tensions, language barriers, isolation and loneliness and worries about citizenship (Gautam, Mawn, and Beehler, 2018). These psychosocial barriers can make some older people feel like they are "aging out of place", hampering integration (Slade and Borovnik, 2018).

Status and family relationships

While family networks can be a source of support, in some cases older people experience a loss of status and independence due to forced migration (Bolzman, 2014; Slade and Borovnik, 2018). For example, research with Syrian grandmothers resettled to Canada revealed that their "authority and status … may be undermined by their comparatively subordinate integration" due to "post-migration configurations of power, care work, and community" (Kahil, Iqbal, and Maghbouleh, 2022). Similarly, a study with older women resettled to Iceland showed how their status changed after migration and their acute awareness of "age and their value or burden in the family" (Dubus, 2018). Research with older South Sudanese migrants also found that their power and influence declined primarily because of their loss of control over the "ownership and management of natural and other resources" (Barbalet, 2018). In some cases, elder abuse and neglect may occur after migration due to family stresses and power inequities (Ploeg, Lohfeld, and Walsh, 2013; Guruge et al., 2021; Sudha and Khadka, 2022).

While the next chapter will cover in more detail changing intergenerational relationships, it is worthwhile noting two key issues here. First, as Slade and Borovnik (2018) argue,

> Instead of experiencing a gradual loss of independence that comes naturally with old age, older refugees experience a sharp and sudden loss that is mainly due to language and cultural barriers. From the moment of resettlement, there is a risk elders may become overwhelmingly dependent on their children and grandchildren for their economic well-being, and for translating and negotiating everyday tasks.

The speed and depth of this dependence on younger generations can have an impact on perceptions and realities of socially constructed roles of authority, leadership, and knowledge ascribed to elders.

Second, migration may cause the physical separation of generations, due to different times and places of displacement, as well as age-specific living arrangements like retirement homes mentioned in the example above. Long-term care facilities for older people may not be able to provide culturally and linguistically appropriate care (Dossa and Coe, 2017). The experiences of Sonya highlighted in the example above are an exception. Because older people are more likely to remain than to move across borders, they can be separated from the rest of their family by time and place. As a result, they are more likely to be involved in transnational family relationships, mediated by information technologies, than non-migrants (Bolzman, 2014).

Health

In addition to the mental health issue highlighted above, the physical health of older refugees may also deteriorate due to the stresses of forced migration and linguistic, financial, and social barriers to accessing health services (Bolzman, 2014). The "exhausted migrant effect" (Bollini and Siem, 1995) describes a rapid decline in health outcomes after migration. A study with older racialized migrants in Europe also highlights "different understandings of care, health, and disease" (Nielsen *et al.*, 2018). These differential understandings are not only cross-cultural but also intergenerational: younger family members may feel stress, and ethical dilemmas in attempting to bridge their older relatives' expectations and needs, and the available resources in the host community (Nielsen *et al.*, 2018).

Language acquisition

Evidence suggests that second language acquisition decreases with age (Singleton, 2001). Older people may have cognitive and physical impediments to learning another language, and/or they may lack the time, social connectiveness, and socialization opportunities to become fluent in the language(s) of the host community (Altinkaya and Omundsen, 1999). On the other hand, a study in Germany suggests that this is sometimes a self-fulling prophesy: "While the language teachers doubt the ability and the readiness of older refugees to learn due to the difficulties that they face, older refugees do not attribute a negative meaning to old age and they do not doubt their ability or their readiness to learn the German language" (Al Ajlan, 2021). Whatever the cause of lower levels of language proficiency, linguistic challenges "can prevent older refugees from accessing important information and services, using public transport, socialising, and ultimately from fostering a sense of belonging in their new society" (Slade and Borovnik, 2018). This isolation, in turn, further reduces opportunities to learn and practice the new language.

Work and retirement

While older people are often assumed to not be actively working, this overlooks their reproductive, often unremunerated, labor in families, communities, and cultural networks (Deneva, 2017). Indeed, some studies have shown that older people come out of retirement after migration due to family care needs, lack of access to financial support and services, and to finance education and businesses of younger generations (VanderPlaat,

Ramos, and Yoshida, 2012; Brotman *et al.*, 2021; Wang and Hari, 2024). However, there are specific barriers to entering the labor market related to immigration status and ageism (Flynn and Wong, 2022), which are exacerbated for older people with limited language.

While Sonya's experiences at the beginning of the chapter show a positive example of Ukrainian refugees accessing culturally appropriate retirement services, this is not the case for all older migrants. Those who have been assigned "bureaucratic birthdates" may find a mismatch between their needs and the artificial chronological age on their identity documents (Nibbs, 2014). This mismatch is exacerbated when birthdates are off by several years, and when older people work in physically demanding jobs (Seibel, 2016b). Because access to state-funded pensions and services in countries of resettlement are based at the intersection of chronological age and migration status, some older refugees do not qualify for social assistance and/or retirement benefits. For some, life in retirement residences does not correspond to cultural expectations of family members caring for them (Bolzman, 2014; Dossa and Coe, 2017).

End-of-life care and death

It is also difficult for older refugees, especially those from religious or cultural minorities, to access culturally appropriate palliative care (Madi *et al.*, 2019). For example, Parin Dossa shows how older Iranian and Ismaili Muslim people in Canada sought dignity and human and spiritual connections in their end-of-life care (Dossa, 2020). People with precarious migration status may not be eligible for state-funded palliative care (Abdelaal, Blake, and Lau, 2021).

Dying in exile poses both practical and emotional challenges. As Bird (2019) recounts from her work with the Karen community in Australia: "Many of its members were old and sick. No-one from the community knew what to do if one passed away in Brisbane or while abroad, visiting dispersed family … [including] the Australian legal and financial requirements after death." The financial costs of funerals and burials may be unknown or out of reach (Bird, 2019), putting further financial and emotional stress on grieving family and community members (Harrell-Bond and Wilson, 1990). People may not have the financial means, immigration status, or immigration documents to travel across borders to attend funerals (Le Gall and Rachédi, 2019). Some cultural and religious rites may not be permitted or practical, and hence have to be adapted (Grønseth, 2018).

Older refugees may be concerned about dying far from their homelands and communities. For example, one Ukrainian refugee said,

> I lived in Bakhmut. It is very difficult for me to speak. Everyone died at my place. We lived on the edge of the street. Now there is nothing left. I was taken by volunteers, what I wear and what I have with me is all that I have left … I am so afraid to die here, I want to go home. I don't know where my relatives are buried. I can't go to the grave. I am 78 years old, I am already an old and sick person. (cited in HelpAge International, 2023a, p. 9)

Others may be concerned that younger generations do not fully understand religious or cultural rituals around death and mourning (Hugman, Bartolomei, and Pittaway, 2004). For example, a 57-year-old Bhutanese refugee in New Zealand said, "Some concern for me is we want to keep our culture alive even though we are in a foreign land … [and] during our death we want that our cremation ceremony and everything should be conducted in our own way, in our cultural way by our children … that is what we want" (Slade and Borovnik, 2018).

Conclusion

This chapter has explored the specific experiences of immobility and migration of older people, who are too often invisible in policy, programming, and research. As aging intersects with other power relations, older migrants face particular health, employment, and retirement challenges. As members of kin, community, and social networks, their migration changes these relationships, as well as socially significant rites of passage, including dying and death.

6
Intergenerational relationships within and across borders

As a human process, migration entails significant changes in inter-personal relationships and power relations at family, community, and societal levels. There is established research on changing gender relations (Hyndman, 2010; Nolin, 2020), but less attention has been paid to social age. This chapter focuses on intergenerational relationships in forced migration contexts across the life course. Using the story of Ilhan Omar, it demonstrates how cross-cultural contexts, as well as the lived experience of forced migration, provoke important changes in social age that affect intersectional power relationships.

Ilhan Omar's story: From refugee to Congresswoman

Ilhan Omar was born in Mogadishu, Somalia, where she lived in the compound of her maternal grandfather, whom she calls Baba. She recalls, "In our Mogadishu compound—filled with

African art, books of history and Somali poetry, and music—the disagreements were constant. We were a multigenerational family—aunties, uncles, cousins, and siblings from my maternal side, all living together" (Omar and Paley, 2020, p. 9). Ilhan's mother died when she was 2 years old, leaving Ilhan and her four older siblings to be raised by Ilhan's father, Baba, and her aunt, whom she called "Habaryar" (literally, "small mom").

War broke out in Mogadishu when Ilhan was 8 years old. She remembers hiding in her father's bedroom "under the bed with my oldest auntie, my habaryar Fos, who had become the only mother I even knew. She was so terrified that she was crying and shaking … I tried to calm her down by talking to her. "Close your eyes and pretend that it's just a movie." (Omar and Paley, 2020, p. 24). The family fled Mogadishu in small groups, with Ilhan's father leaving first with her two eldest siblings, who were deemed most at risk. She left with her aunt and arrived in Kismayo, a Somali port city, where they stayed a few months. Finally, Ilhan's grandfather arrived. The family then all crossed into Kenya at different times and by different methods—foot, boat, and small plane.

They lived in a refugee camp, where Ilhan's habaryar Fos died of malaria, as did other extended family members. She recalls, "I didn't worry about myself as much as I worried about my dad, whose immune system wasn't strong enough to protect him from malaria. He got sick all the time" (Omar and Paley, 2020, p. 41). When UNHCR contacted the family about resettlement options, Ilhan asked her father, "Are we all going to go together? Because I don't want to go anywhere without you or Baba" (Omar and Paley, 2020, p. 54). But her grandfather had a separate resettlement file, so Ilhan, her father, and siblings were resettled to the US first. They arrived in Arlington, Virginia. Her grandfather was later resettled to Minnesota.

Ilhan's family moved to Minneaopolis in 1997. "Living in Minneapolis was great for me, because I now had all these relatives I could visit" (cited in Omar and Paley, 2020, p. 85). She often stayed with her single uncle or her grandfather. Her older sister "mothered" her, creating tensions: "We fought all the time because she didn't understand the typically American teenage tendencies I was developing. 'Leave me alone; I want my space' has no place in the traditional Somali family, where it is normal for everyone to be in your business and for you to care what they thought" (Omar and Paley, 2020, p. 85).

Ilhan accompanied her grandfather to political meetings to interpret for him. She became a US citizen in 2000, when she was 17. In 2016, she was elected to the Minnesota House of Representatives. In 2018, she ran in Minnesota's 5th congressional district and, in 2019, she was sworn in as to the US House of Representatives.

Ilhan's story highlights different and dynamic concepts of family as people migrate, and how these family relationships adapt to different cultural and social contexts. As in Ilhan's case, migration may entail family separation—temporarily or permanently—but relationships are maintained across borders and reconfigured through different media. Intergenerational power relations also change over time and space, as people age across the life course in dynamic forced migration contexts.

Shifting definitions of family and kin networks

One significant point highlighted by Ilhan's story is the differential conceptualization and definitions of family relationships across host states of asylum, but also within different communities. Most resettlement and asylum policies in Global North countries define family narrowly as the nuclear family: spouses and dependent children, often under a certain chronological age. The definition of spouse has expanded in recent years to include same-sex marriages and conjugal relationships outside marriage. However, a similar expansion in relation to social age has not occurred. Generally speaking, Global North countries only recognize biological or legally adopted children under the age of 18, with some allowing for inclusion of older children with disabilities who still rely financially on their parents. As discussed in the previous chapter, this concept of dependence overlooks interdependent relationships. In Ilhan's example above, she comforted her aunt, worried about her father's health, and interpreted for her grandfather.

The narrow nuclear family definition also overlooks extended, intergenerational relationships that constitute family in many cultures and in the context of violence, death, and displacement (Ayika *et al.*, 2018). As Balakian (2023) argues,

> Aunts and other kin act as primary caregivers for children who are orphaned or separated from biogenetic parents. Yet, state and non-governmental bureaucracies that manage refugee resettlement use the biogenetic, nuclear family as a standard for resettlement and

family reunification. People whose networks of social care exceed the boundaries of the nuclear family face an extra burden of proving their families are legitimate.

In Ilhan's story, her aunt acted as her "small mom" after Ilhan's mother died, but there was no formal adoption, as her father was still alive. As also demonstrated by Ilhan's story, grandparents are often part of intergenerational, interdependent living and caring arrangements, but are not considered to be part of the family for resettlement purposes in Global North countries. Research indicates that this creates stress and/or separation within families, as grandparents are left behind while the nuclear family is resettled (Dubus, 2018). Not all are as fortunate as Ilhan and her Baba were to be resettled to the same country, albeit to different states and at different times.

As families migrate to contexts where family is defined differently, they may feel disadvantaged. For example, research with families who migrated to Australia demonstrates that they lose social capital when they move to a country that focuses on individual achievement and the nuclear family (Wali and Renzaho, 2018). One Burmese participant in a focus group said, "For women it's hard to manage everything so if someone works, wants to earn money and bring home the money and then she has to manage everything around the house. Back home there were grandparents, aunties, uncles and they were all around the corner which wasn't too far" (cited in Wali and Renzaho, 2018). Similarly, Ilhan's family moved from Virginia to Minnesota to be closer to extended family and Somali kinship networks.

Transnational families

In contexts of forced migration, some families become separated across borders, resulting in transnational kinship structures. Ilhan's extended family fled at different times within Somalia, and then across the border to Kenya. Due to the US refugee resettlement program's definition of family, extended families area often separated (Grace, 2019). For example, if Ilhan's aunt, who was her surrogate mother, had not died, she still would not have been able to be resettled with Ilhan. Similarly, Ilhan's grandfather had to complete a separate resettlement application despite his instrumental role in Ilhan's care and upbringing.

As a result, families need to adapt to maintaining kinship ties across borders. Some use information communication technologies to sustain relationships (Bacigalupe and Cámara, 2012). Many send financial remittances home to family members left behind in countries of origin or asylum to maintain reciprocal kinship networks (Lindley, 2009). Research with refugees in Australia indicates that "sending money home was an additional stressful responsibility and an obligation because participants recalled that their family had supported them while they needed it the most" (Wali and Renzaho, 2018).

Transnational relationships also in some cases lead to family sponsorship or "chain migration", where "transnational social and familial networks … are constantly being renewed through ties of kinship, love, obligation, reciprocity and identity" (Ní Laoire, 2023). In some cases, this family reunification is explicitly or implicitly related to expanding access to childcare and other familial supports (Westcott and Robertson, 2017; Bélanger and

Candiz, 2020), again demonstrating mutual interdependence within families.

Social age and changing intergenerational power relations

As explained in Chapter 1, because age and aging are socially constructed, they vary depending on time and place. Forced migration not only entails a change to a new social environment, but also has differential impacts across the life course, as demonstrated in Chapters 2 to 5. This means that people in situations of forced migration encounter different socially constructed notions of life course categories, but also experience changes in their own intergenerational relationships at interpersonal, family, community, and societal levels.

One key change that happens with migration is the infantilization of adults and adultification of children. As explained in Chapters 2 and 3, children and young people may adapt more quickly to a new country (Morantz, Rousseau, and Heymann, 2012) and become settlement "champions" for their families (Shakya *et al.*, 2014). At the same time, adults and older people may experience deskilling and language and integration challenges that render them socially less powerful. In some cases, this results in role reversal. As one refugee said, "I feel like her daughter not her mother" (Dubus, 2010). These role changes can create tensions (McMichael, Gifford, and Correa-Velez, 2011). For example, a participant in a focus group in Australia reported, ""Sorry. In Syria, they were more respectable to their parents. In Australia, they don't care, and sometimes they don't respect me or my thoughts or their father's thoughts. At the same time, sometimes I will be talking to them about something, they leave me talking and go away…" (Ayika *et al.*, 2018).

Layered on these changing intergenerational power relations are dynamic approaches to parenting due to different norms, social structures, and expectations in countries of asylum and resettlement (Deng and Marlowe, 2013). Bejenaru's (2018) research shows how parents in migration contexts draw on both their own childhoods, but also social cues in the host countries to negotiate and adjust child-rearing and familial relationships. Parenting is often the site at which both adults and children "navigate and integrate the values of two cultures" (Cook and Waite, 2016). As one woman remarked, "And there's a barrier here, when they learn these things and they come back home, we do discipline our children but the law will tell you can't even discipline them here …" (Ayika *et al.*, 2018).

As shown in the previous chapter, older people may experience a loss of status and social networks. For example, Ilhan's grandfather was the center of the intergenerational compound in Mogadishu and was a key figure in her upbringing. However, he had to resettle separately from the rest of the family in the US. While he remained important in Ilhan's life, she increasingly took care of him, serving as an interpreter, for example.

Intergenerational distance across time and space

Due to housing availability, costs, and regulations, intergenerational families who lived together in their country of origin may be housed only with nuclear families in countries of asylum and resettlement. For example, Ilhan lived in an intergenerational compound in Somalia, but only with her father and siblings in the US. Research indicates that this is common as household compositions adapt to new social norms in countries of the Global North (McMichael, Gifford, and Correa-Velez, 2011).

In addition to fewer opportunities for intergenerational living, age- and generation-specific programming with rigid chrono-logical age categories also separates intergenerational groups. For example, settlement agencies often limit "youth" and "senior" programming to specific chronological ages that may not align with life experiences (Clark-Kazak, 2025). Physical distances between family members as well as lifestyle changes that require more time at work, in language training, and formal education means there are fewer opportunities for impromptu gatherings and interactions (Wali and Renzaho, 2018). As one Iraqi refugee said, "There is no social life. There is no family. You can't find enough time to talk to your own children or to share their life" (Wali and Renzaho, 2018).

On the other hand, research also indicates reciprocity—sometimes across time—in kin relationships (Dossa and Coe, 2017, p. 13). As Ni Laoire (2023) argues, "[M]igrations and mobili-ties are experienced and reproduced intergenerationally, in ways that connect past, present and future generations within fami-lies. The consequences of past migrations reverberate, often in unpredictable ways, across multiple generations." We will return to the temporal aspect of intergenerational relationships in the next chapter.

Conclusion

This chapter has demonstrated how families are differentially defined in different countries and societies, resulting in dynamic conceptualizations of kinship across borders. The narrow focus on nuclear families in my countries of asylum and resettlement in the Global South both restricts access to these opportunities for extended family members, but also changes the nature of familial relations, including parenting, after migration. A social age lens helps to understand these intergenerational power relations and their intersectionality with gender and other positionalities.

7
Looking to the future: Centering time and aging in forced migration research, policy, and programming

This chapter shows how social age is related to new theories of time in forced migration. It demonstrates how aging in forced migration contexts is a crucial analytical lens, which, along with other intersecting power relationships, must be understood to appreciate the complexities of forced migration experiences. In particular, chronometric time is central to immigration processes, but, despite its apparent neutrality, has differential impacts on people at different stages of the life course and in different intergenerational relationships. Picking up on the key threads of chronological age, temporality, and generations, I provide recommendations for forced migration research, policy, and programming.

Jaivet Ealom's experiences of immigration detention

Jaivet Ealom is a Muslim Rohingya, born in Maungdaw, Burma, on the border of Bangladesh. He recalls his mother or grandmother explaining the world to him as follows: "You young guys are like tadpoles swimming in the hoofprint of a bull" (Ealom, 2022). While Jaivet shared a common identity of Muslim Rohingya with older generations, the latter "had the good fortune of being born in an earlier era of relative security. My grandparents remembered being able to travel wherever they liked. They lived a life of freedom and choices. My brother, Shahed, and I—also born in Burma—did not" (Ealom, 2022).

Jaivet was admitted into a university program at Dagon University in Ragoon. While he was there, Rohingya villages in his home state were attacked and burned. Jaivet fled to Indonesia, where he lived with another Rohingya family and registered for an appointment with UNHCR, scheduled for 2.5 months later. When he found out that Rohingya were waiting years for resettlement, he paid smugglers for a spot on a boat to Christmas Island, an Australian offshore territory. There, he was detained at the Christmas Island Immigration Detention Centre. After several days, Jaivet was sent to a prison on Manus Island in Papua New Guinea (PNG), which he describes as "a lawless, chaotic human zoo" (Ealom, 2022).

> When I looked around the compound, I saw hundreds of intelligent men in the prime of their lives being deliberately trampled. Like me, a lot of guys were in their 20s—a time when we should have been setting the

foundations for our later years. I worried that, if my 20s were lost in offshore detention, I would become permanently isolated from the world. It would take a heroic effort—maybe an impossible one—to be "normal" again. (Ealom, 2022)

In 2016, the PNG Supreme Court ruled that immigration detention was unconstitutional. While the detainees were legally allowed to leave, practically there was no way for them to get off the island: "The gates were open, but we were as confined as ever. We had no place to go and no hope of employment in Lorengau" (Ealom, 2022). Jaivet disguised himself as an interpreter and took a flight to Solomon Islands, before eventually making it to Canada, where he claimed asylum.

Temporality permeates Jaivet's multiple displacements within and across borders. He experienced life in Myanmar differently than his mother and grandmother, showing the importance of generational relationships and changes over time. His life in exile is permeated by waiting: for UNHCR, for asylum decisions, inside the repetitive life of immigration detention. And he experienced the uncertainties of indefinite detention, which, even when rendered illegal, still confined him on Manus Island. This chapter addresses the emerging research on time and forced migration from a social age perspective and highlights recurring themes throughout the book.

Significance of chronometric time in migration policies

As we have seen in all chapters, chronometric time is significant in migration polices, programming, and laws. From birth, a person's chronological age accords protections, rights, and privileges in countries of resettlement ordered by chronometric time and (bureaucratic) birthdates. As an ostensibly objective means of inclusion and exclusion, birthdates are rarely questioned, even as they are acknowledged to be, in some cases, fictions created by UNHCR officers. Endorsed—time and time again—by immigration officials, educators, healthcare workers, tax administrators, and gatekeepers, birthdates determine access to age-specific programs, services, and activities. Indelibly imprinted on identity documents, (bureaucratic) birthdates take on administrative and social significance. They also directly impact on displaced people's everyday lives: "Time moves immigrant children in and out of legal categories and legalization channels" (Gonzales, 2016, p. 18).

As Cohen (2018) has argued, time has specific political value and significance in immigration processes, where the duration of residence determines eligibility for permanent residence and citizenship. Visas and asylum procedures are time-bound, requiring people to "periodically renew their documents and make sure they are up-to-date with the temporal demands of their country of asylum" (Tefera, 2021). Similarly, states regularly advertise immigration processing times. However, unlike the severe legal consequences for overstaying a visa or not responding to immigration requirements by due dates, governments may or may not respect processing times, with little recourse for those whose lives hang in the balance. As Griffiths (2014) argues,

> One temporal consideration, that of speed, is a particularly contentious aspect of the immigration system. There are competing claims that the system is too fast and too slow: that the wheels of the system turn so

slowly that people wait years for decisions, but also that decisions are rushed, with decisions in the Detained Fast Track, for example, being made in just a few days.

Durational time is also normally significant in criminal justice penalties, where people "serve time" depending on the gravity of their crime. However, in immigration detention, which falls under administrative law, detention is often indefinite, as demonstrated by Jaivet's experiences. Western liberal democracies profiled in this book—Canada, the US, the UK, Germany, and Australia—all regularly detain immigrants, sometimes for years at a time, even if they have committed no crime.

The passage of time can change immigration law and policy from one day to the next. As demonstrated in Jaivet's story, the PNG court decision made immigration detention illegal. Democratically elected government respond to public opinion that is more or less favorable to immigration at any given time and in response to domestic and international events, resulting in significant policy changes that can be enacted quickly. For example, US President Biden and the Canadian Prime Minister Trudeau announced significant changes to the Safe Third Country Agreement—which effectively blocked asylum seekers from claiming refuge in the other country— on a Friday night, with the changes in effect a few hours later, as of midnight on Saturday, March 25, 2023. Asylum seekers already enroute to the US-Canada border arrived minutes too late and were turned away (Stevenson, 2023). These dynamic political contexts, combined with seasonal weather patterns, means that many people "wait for the 'right' time in an attempt to cross borders or seek asylum" (Tefera, 2021).

The significance of durational time varies depending on chronological age, social age, and life course. Five years can be all of a young child's life. It can also represent the last years of an older person's life. Jaivet highlights the emotional toll of being detained in his 20s, "a time when we should have been setting the foundations for our later years" (Ealom, 2022). As shown in Chapter 3, people may delay or accelerate life course decisions like marriage or childbirth, depending on the timing and family-related restrictions of immigration policies.

Temporality and (im)mobility

In contrast to the exactness implied by chronometric time, people in contexts of forced migration may experience temporality differently because of their (im)mobility. As Jaivet writes,

> Time was elastic on Manus Island. It twisted and elongated according to the state of sadness or physical pain you were in. Years of lining up for food three times a day had homogenized existence to a point where each hour merged with the next. We were stuck in a continuous moment: a line that rotated in a pointless circle with no terminus. (Ealom, 2022)

The indefiniteness of immigration detention has been equated to torture (Arbel and Davis, 2018; Silverman, 2024). Moreover, even short periods of time in immigration detention have been shown to have disproportionately negative impacts on children and young people's physical, emotional, and psychological development (Cox, 2009; Kronick, Rousseau, and Cleveland, 2018; Triggs, 2018).

As alluded to in Chapter 3, the uncertainty and instability of being "forced into a state of limbo, immobility and waiting [through] … restrictive bordering and migration management" (Tefera, 2021) leads to "wasted time", especially for people at significant life course transitions (Grabska, 2020). People who are waiting for immigration decisions may feel "stalled" (Fee, 2022) or "stuck" in temporal limbo, where time is frozen for them, but not for others. For example, a young undocumented person in the US said, "I feel as though I've experienced this weird psychological and legal stunted growth. I'm stuck at sixteen, like a clock that has stopped ticking. My life has not changed at all since then. Although I'm twenty-two, I feel like a kid. I can't do anything adults do" (Cory, cited in Gonzales, 2016, pp. 100–101). Similarly, a Kurdish man (cited in Griffiths, 2014) whose asylum claim had been refused, but who had not yet had a deportation order, lamented, "My case, it's been like stuck for six years. Six years! Six years with no answer!"

The concept of "violent uncertainty" has been developed to highlight how insecure immigration status can cause direct and indirect harms and deleterious health outcomes (Phillimore and Cheung, 2021). For example, one man who had been waiting eight years for an immigration decision in the UK described the stress of living in "a parallel universe" as a "forgotten" undocumented migrant: "Look at my hair! No hair over just one piece of paper. A piece of paper!" (Griffiths, 2014). The physical and mental health implications of "violent uncertainty" vary depending on social age and life course, as demonstrated in Chapters 3 and 5 on young and older people, respectively. Shakhsari (2014) contends that the "time of refugee rights" is what Berlant (2007) conceptualizes as "slow death". They write, "living with specters of the past, present, and future is not just to live with the memory of those who are no longer present, but with the ghostly presence of living refugees who are not organized into the realm of remembering and documentation".

Despite the constraints imposed by (im)mobility, people in contexts of migration do create their own rhythm of life, "punctuated by repeated patterns and routines of everyday life, the timings, durations, and regularities, which can shape and sustain a sense of place for individuals and communities" (Tefera, 2021). Life goes on. Whole generations are born, grow up, marry, have children, and die in long-standing refugee camps symptomatic of protracted displacement. The routine of the detention center on Manus Island allowed Jaivet to be able to escape by observing the rhythm of guard changes.

Generations and social age

As shown at the beginning of Jaivet's story, he experienced being a persecuted Rohingya in Myanmar differently than his mother and grandmother, who grew up in different eras. Throughout this book, I have also demonstrated how different generations have differential migration experiences even as they live in the same time and place. As discussed in Chapter 2, children born in exile may have different citizenship, but also different experiences of childhood and youth than their parents. Migration studies has historically referred to first-, 1.5-, and second-generation immigrants to separate out different cohorts who were born outside the country of residence; came to the country as children; and were born in the country but to parents born abroad, respectively. However, the notion of "generation" is somewhat of a misnomer as siblings may be categorized in different migration generations, as in the example of Eyad in Chapter 2.

Social age analysis pays particular attention to intra- and intergenerational power relations, and how these intersect with gender, sexuality, religion, class, ability, race, ethnicity, etc. Generational relationships in contexts of migration span both time and space. Moreover, as Thelen and Coe argue, migration sometimes implies "temporalities of reciprocity across the life course" (Thelen and Coe, 2019). A common motivation for migration—both forced and voluntary—is to provide a better future for one's children. In contexts of reciprocal and interdependent kin and family relationships, researchers, practitioners and policymakers need to better take into account these realities.

Social age and life course analysis in forced migration work

In this concluding chapter, I would like to end with a few recommendations to make forced migration studies, policy and programming more age sensitive. First, *all* initiatives should require a social age analysis, whether or not they are explicitly intended for a specific age category. As demonstrated throughout this book, as an inherently human process, migration is experienced differently depending on social age, chronological age, family status, and life course. Ignoring this important fact of life means that research, policy, and programming is at best age-insensitive and at worst ageist. As I have argued elsewhere (Clark-Kazak, 2009), a social age analysis requires age-disaggregated statistics, understandings of locally specific conceptualizations of aging across the life course, and attention to how power inequities related to life course intersect with other positionalities.

A second, related point, is the need for a more holistic understanding of age beyond chronology. Forced migration research, policy, and programming is dominated by chronological age categories that serve to further label, border, and restrict access to services. Ageist assumptions and language are also regularly encountered in forced migration discourse (Clark-Kazak, 2016; 2025). A better understanding of the ways in which age is socially constructed—including in countries ordered by chronometric time—would help to displace problematic ideas of neutrality and universality of chronological age and center differential lived experiences across the life course.

Third, more research is required to better understand the needs and experiences of older people in contexts of forced migration. We have very little data—both quantitative and qualitative—on older people's displacement experiences. On a related note, governments and refugee-serving organizations should provide more practical information on legal and health requirements surrounding death in countries of reception. There should also be more supports in place for minority religious and cultural groups to adapt their end-of-life, funeral and mourning rituals to the laws and policies in place in countries of asylum and resettlement.

Notes

1. I am grateful to Nour Halabi for her early enthusiasm for this book and for helping me to conceptualize the "cradle-to-grave" arc it has taken.

2. The Private sponsorship of Refugees (PSR) program is a unique initiative that allows Canadian residents and permanent residents to sponsor refugees to resettle to Canada as permanent residents.

3. A natural experiment refers to a situation where a certain group of people are exposed to a particular policy, program, or event—in this case DACA—while others (the control group) are not. This allows researchers to compare outcomes for those exposed to the phenomenon to the control group to determine the consequences of the policy, program, or event.

4. *Travaux préparatoires* refer to documents relating to negotiations of treaties. They help to indicate the intention of the treaty drafters.

Recommended projects/ assignments/ discussion questions

1. Assignment: Analysis of a news article on forced migration

    Read a recent news article on forced migration in your community/country. Does it include age-disaggregated information? If so, what does this tell you about differential experiences of migration across the life course in this context? If not, what information would you like to know to better understand social age and migration? How would/ does social age analysis enrich your understanding of this example of forced migration?

2. Project: Case study analysis of a migration project

    Choose one of the examples of a migration project below. To what extent does the project acknowledge different age categories and life course experiences? What perspectives are missing? What more information would you need to do a comprehensive social age analysis? What recommendations would you offer the organization to make the project more age sensitive?

IOM. Families of missing migrations project.

https://missingmigrants.iom.int/families-missing-migrants

Terre des hommes. SMILE: Support for displaced Ukrainian children.

https://tdh-ukraine.org/en/smile-support-children-and-their-families-during-migration-and-integration-new-local-environments

Older adult refugees and friends project.

https://drcog.org/programs/area-agency-aging/older-adult-refugees-and-friends-program

3. Discussion question: In your view, why are social age and life course considerations not more systematically integrated into forced migration research, policy, and programming? What would you recommend to encourage more age-sensitive approaches?

4. Discussion question: What do you think governments should do when people in situations of forced migration lack documentation, like birth certificates, to prove their chronological age?

References

Abdelaal, M., Blake, C. and Lau, J. (2021). Challenges of Providing Palliative and End-of-Life Care to Refugee Claimants in Canada: A Case Report. *Journal of Palliative Medicine*, 24(4), pp. 635–638. Available at: https://doi.org/10.1089/jpm.2020.0422.

Aberman, T. (2014.). Gendered Perspectives on Refugee Determination in Canada. *Refuge: Canada's Journal on Refugees*, 30(2), pp. 57–66. Available at: https://doi.org/10.25071/1920-7336.39619.

Aberman, T. (forthcoming). (Re)Conceptualizing Gender and Sexuality: Current Understandings and Debates in Forced Migration Research and Policy in Canada. In: *Forced Migration in/to Canada: From Colonization to Refugee Resettlement*. MQUP.

d'Abreu, A., Castro-Olivo, S. and Ura, S. K. (2019). Understanding the Role of Acculturative Stress on Refugee Youth Mental Health: A Systematic Review and Ecological Approach to Assessment and Intervention. *School Psychology International*, 40(2), pp. 107–127. Available at: https://doi.org/10.1177/0143034318822688.

AGE Platform Europe (2024n.d.). Ukraine: the "oldest" humanitarian crisis in the world. Available at: https://www.age-platform.eu/ukraine-the-oldest-humanitarian-crisis-in-the-world/.

Al Ajlan, A. (2021). Older Refugees in Germany: What Are the Reasons for the Difficulties in Language-learning? *Journal of Refugee Studies*, 34(2), pp. 2449–2465. Available at: https://doi.org/10.1093/jrs/fez056.

Altinkaya, J. and Omundsen, H. (1999). "Birds in a Gilded Cage": Resettlement Prospects for Adult Refugees in New Zealand. *Social Policy Journal of New Zealand* [Preprint], (13).

Available at: https://www.msd.govt.nz/about-msd-and-our-work/publications-resources/journals-and-magazines/social-pol icy-journal/spj13/birds-in-a-gilded-cage-resettlement-prospe cts-for-adult-refugees.html.

Amanpour, C. (2023). After fleeing Taliban rule, Zahra Joya is shining a light on the struggles of Afghanistan's women. *CNN*, September 19. Available at: https://www.cnn.com/videos/tv/ 2023/09/19/cfc-amanpour-zahra-joya.cnn.

Antony-Newman, M. and Niyozov, S. (2023). Barriers and Facilitators for Academic Success and Social Integration of Refugee Students in Canadian and US K–12 Schools: A Meta-Synthesis. *Canadian Journal of Education/Revue canadienne de l'éducation* [Preprint]. Available at: https://doi.org/10.53967/ cje-rce.5859.

Arbel, E. and Davis, I. C. (2018). Immigration Detention and the Problem of Time: Lessons from Solitary Confinement. *International Journal of Migration and Border Studies*, 4(4), p. 326. Available at: https://doi.org/10.1504/IJMBS.2018.096775.

Arendt, Hannah. 1943. We Refugees. *Menorah Journal* 31, no. 1 (1943): 69-77.

Ayika, D. *et al.* (2018). A Qualitative Exploration of Post-Migration Family Dynamics and Intergenerational Relationships. *SAGE Open*, 8(4), 215824401881175. Available at: https://doi.org/10.1177/ 2158244018811752.

Bacigalupe, G. and Cámara, M. (2012). Transnational Families and Social Technologies: Reassessing Immigration Psychology. *Journal of Ethnic and Migration Studies*, 38(9), pp. 1425–1438. Available at: https://doi.org/10.1080/1369183X.2012.698211.

Bajwa, J. K., Abai, M., Kidd, S., Couto, S., Akbari-Dibavar, A. and McKenzie, K. (2018). Examining the Intersection of Race, Gender, Class, and Age on Post-Secondary Education and Career Trajectories of Refugees. *Refuge*, 34(2), pp. 113–123.

Balakian, S. (2023). Of Aunts and Mothers: Refugee Resettlement, the Nuclear Family, and Caring for "Other" Children in Kenya. *Ethnic and Racial Studies*, 46(2), pp. 213–232. Available at: https://doi.org/10.1080/01419870.2022.2063693.

Banerjee, R., Reitz, J. G. and Oreopoulos, P. (2018). Do Large Employers Treat Racial Minorities More Fairly? An Analysis of Canadian Field Experiment Data. *Canadian Public Policy*, 44(1), pp. 1–12. Available at: https://doi.org/10.3138/cpp.2017-033.

Banerjee, R. (2022). Time to Change Focus? A Review of Immigrant Labour Market Barriers, Outcomes and the Role of Employers in Canada. *Institute for Canadian Citizenship*. Available at: https://inclusion.ca/wp-content/uploads/2022/11/TimeToChangeFocus_ICC.pdf.

Barbalet, V. (2018). Older People in Displacement: Falling through the Cracks of Emergency Responses. ODI Institute. Available at: https://media.odi.org/documents/12292.pdf.

Bauer, E. (2016). Practising Kinship Care: Children as Language Brokers in Migrant Families. *Childhood*, 23(1), pp. 22–36. Available at: https://doi.org/10.1177/0907568215574917.

Behtoui, A. (2021). Constructions of Self-identification: Children of Immigrants in Sweden. *Identities*, 28(3), pp. 341–360. Available at: https://doi.org/10.1080/1070289X.2019.1658396.

Bejenaru, A. (2018). Immigration, Transition to Parenthood, and Parenting. In: I. Vlase and B. Voicu, eds., *Gender, Family, and Adaptation of Migrants in Europe*. Cham: Springer International Publishing, pp. 141–169. Available at: https://doi.org/10.1007/978-3-319-76657-7_7.

Bélanger, D. and Candiz, G. (2020). The Politics of "Waiting" for Care: Immigration Policy and Family Reunification in Canada. *Journal of Ethnic and Migration Studies; Abingdon*, 46(16), pp. 3472–3490. Available at: http://dx.doi.org.proxy.bib.uottawa.ca/10.1080/1369183X.2019.1592399.

Bélanger, D. and Haemmerli, G. (2019). "We no longer fear brides from afar": Marriage Markets and Gendered Mobilities in Rural

Vietnam. *Asian and Pacific Migration Journal*, 28(3), pp. 245–270. Available at: https://doi.org/10.1177/0117196819869060.

Bélanger, D. and Silvey, R. (2020). An Im/mobility Turn: Power Geometries of Care and Migration. *Journal of Ethnic and Migration Studies*, 46(16), pp. 3423–3440. Available at: https://doi.org/10.1080/1369183X.2019.1592396.

Berlant, L. (2007). Slow Death (Sovereignty, Obesity, Lateral Agency). *Critical Inquiry*, 33(4), pp. 754–780. Available at: https://doi.org/10.1086/521568.

Bhabha, J. (2004). Demography and Rights: Women, Children and Access to Asylum. *International Journal of Refugee Law*, 16(2), pp. 227–243. Available at: https://doi.org/10.1093/ijrl/16.2.227.

Bhabha, J. (2009). Arendt's Children: Do Today's Migrant Children Have a Right to Have Rights? *Human Rights Quarterly*, 31(2), pp. 410–451. Available at: https://doi.org/10.1353/hrq.0.0072.

Bialas, U. (2023). *Forever 17: Coming of Age in the German Asylum System*. Ethnographic encounters and discoveries. Chicago and London: The University of Chicago Press.

Bird, J. N. (2019). Death and Dying in a Karen Refugee Community: An Overlooked Challenge in the Resettlement Process. *Ethnography*, 20(4), pp. 443–462. Available at: https://doi.org/10.1177/1466138118768624.

Bollini, P. and Siem, H. (1995). No Real Progress Towards Equity: Health of Migrants and Ethnic Minorities on the Eve of the Year 2000. *Social Science & Medicine*, 41(6), pp. 819–828. Available at: https://doi.org/10.1016/0277-9536(94)00386-8.

Bolzman, C. (2014). Older Refugees. In: E. Fiddian-Qasmiyeh *et al.*, eds., *The Oxford Handbook of Refugee and Forced Migration Studies*. Oxford: Oxford University Press. Available at: https://doi.org/10.1093/oxfordhb/9780199652433.013.0039.

Bora, A. (2022). Platforms supporting Ukrainian refugees must prioritise their safety—or risk exposing them to trafficking and exploitation. *The Conversation*, April 11. Available at: https://thec onversation.com/platforms-supporting-ukrainian-refugees-must-prioritise-their-safety-or-risk-exposing-them-to-trafficking-and-exploitation-180967.

Bove, C. and Sharmahd, N. (2020). Beyond Invisibility. Welcoming Children and Families with Migrant and Refugee Background in ECEC Settings. *European Early Childhood Education Research Journal*, 28(1), pp. 1–9. Available at: https://doi.org/10.1080/1350293X.2020.1707940.

Brotman, S. *et al.* (2021). Intergenerational Care in the Context of Migration: A Feminist Intersectional Life-Course Exploration of Racialized Young Adult Women's Narratives of Care. *Affilia*, 36(4), pp. 552–570. Available at: https://doi.org/10.1177/0886109920954408.

Burfitt, P. (2023). Refugee mother says giving birth in Wollongong Hospital one of most traumatic experiences of her life. *ABC Illawarra*, August 15. Available at: https://www.abc.net.au/news/2023-08-15/refugee-births-australia-dire-birth-trauma/102709078.

Burgard, A. (2021). Contested Childhood: Assessing the Age of Young Refugees in the Aftermath of the Second World War. *History Workshop Journal*, 92, pp. 174–193. Available at: https://doi.org/10.1093/hwj/dbab016.

Carcamo, C. (2019). Love in the time of DACA. *LA Times*, December 30. Available at: https://www.latimes.com/california/story/2019-12-30/when-do-you-reveal-your-legal-status-love-in-the-time-of-daca.

Carver, N. (2021). *Marriage, Gender, and Refugee Migration: Spousal Relationships among Somali Muslims in the UK*. Politics of marriage and gender: global issues in local contexts. New Brunswick: Rutgers University Press.

Charsley, K. *et al.* (2020). *Marriage Migration and Integration*. Palgrave Macmillan studies in family and intimate life. Cham: Palgrave Macmillan.

Cheatham, A. and Roy, D. (2023). US Detention of Child Migrants. Council on Foreign Relations. Available at: https://www.cfr. org/backgrounder/us-detention-child-migrants#:~:text= Immigration%20authorities%20encountered%20more%20t han,also%20detained%20infants%20and%20toddlers.

Cherri, Z. *et al.* (2017). Early Marriage and Barriers to Contraception among Syrian Refugee Women in Lebanon: A Qualitative Study. *International Journal of Environmental Research and Public Health*, 14(8), p. 836. Available at: https://doi.org/10.3390/ijerph1 4080836.

Ciufo, D. (forthcoming). Advancing Children's Right to Migration in Canada: Assessing the Participatory Rights of Unaccompanied Minors in their Refugee Claim Process. *The International Journal of Children's Rights* [Preprint].

Clark, C. R. (2008). Understanding Vulnerability: From Categories to Experiences of Young Congolese People in Uganda. *Children & Society*, 21(4), pp. 284–296. Available at: https://doi.org/10.1111/ j.1099-0860.2007.00100.x.

Clark-Kazak, C. (2009a). Representing Refugees in the Life Cycle: A Social Age Analysis of United Nations High Commissioner for Refugees Annual Reports and Appeals 1999–2008. *Journal of Refugee Studies*, 22(3), pp. 302–322. Available at: https://doi.org/ 10.1093/jrs/fep012.

Clark-Kazak, C. (2009b). Towards a Working Definition and Application of Social Age in International Development Studies. *Journal of Development Studies*, 45(8), pp. 1307–1324. Available at: https://doi.org/10.1080/00220380902862952.

Clark-Kazak, C. (2011). *Recounting Migration: Political Narratives of Congolese young people in Uganda*. Montreal and Kingston: McGill-Queen's Press-MQUP.

Clark-Kazak, C. (2012). The Politics of Formal Schooling in Refugee Contexts: Education, Class, and Decision Making among Congolese in Uganda. *Refuge: Canada's Journal on*

Refugees, 27(2), pp. 57–64. Available at: https://doi.org/10.25071/1920-7336.34722.

Clark-Kazak, C. (2016). Mainstreaming Social Age in the Sustainable Development Goals: Progress, Pitfalls, and Prospects. In: R. Huijsmans, ed., *Generationing Development: A Relational Approach to Children, Youth and Development*. London: Palgrave Macmillan UK, pp. 103–124. Available at: https://doi.org/10.1057/978-1-137-55623-3_5.

Clark-Kazak, C. (2022). Family separations in Ukraine highlight the importance of children's rights. *The Conversation*, March 20. Available at: https://theconversation.com/family-separations-in-ukraine-highlight-the-importance-of-childrens-rights-179131.

Clark-Kazak, C. (2025). *Social Age and Immigration Policy in Canada: Towards an Equitable Approach*. University of British Columbia Press.

Clark-Kazak, C. (2009). Towards a Working Definition and Application of Social Age in International Development Studies. *Journal of Development Studies*, 45(8), pp. 1307–1324. Available at: https://doi.org/10.1080/00220380902862952.

Clark-Kazak, C. (2013). Theorizing Age and Generation in Migration Contexts: Towards Social Age Mainstreaming?. *Canadian Ethnic Studies*, 44(3), pp. 1–10. Available at: https://doi.org/10.1353/ces.2013.0009.

Clark-Kazak, C. (Forthcoming). Unaccompanied Minors in the Borderlands: Suspicions and Assumptionsat the Intersection of Gender and Social Age. *Routledge Companion to Gender and Borderlands*, edited by Zalfa Feghali and Deborah Toner. London: Routledge.

Cohen, E. F. (2018). *The Political Value of Time: Citizenship, Duration, and Democratic Justice*. 1st edn. Cambridge University Press. Available at: https://doi.org/10.1017/9781108304283.

Congressional Research Service (2021). Deferred Action for Childhood Arrivals (DACA): By the Numbers. Available at: https://sgp.fas.org/crs/homesec/R46764.pdf.

Contrera, J. (2019). She must choose: Stay with her undocumented family in America or live freely in Canada. *Washington Post*, July 26. Available at: https://www.washingtonpost.com/local/she-must-choose-stay-with-her-undocumented-family-in-america-or-live-freely-in-canada/2019/07/26/b1938cd2-9ce7-11e9-b27f-ed2942f73d70_story.html.

Cook, J. and Waite, L. (2016). 'I think I'm more free with them'— Conflict, Negotiation and Change in Intergenerational Relations in African Families Living in Britain. *Journal of Ethnic and Migration Studies*, 42(8), pp. 1388–1402. Available at: https://doi.org/10.1080/1369183X.2015.1073578.

Costello, C., Nalule, C. and Ozkul, D. (2020). Recognising Refugees: Understanding the Real Routes to Recognition. *Forced Migration Review* [Preprint], (65). Available at: https://www.fmreview.org/recognising-refugees/costello-nalule-ozkul.

Cowper-Smith, Y. and Kane, J. (2024). The shifting landscape of statelessness in Canada. In: *Forced migration in/to Canada: From colonization to refugee resettlement*. Montreal and Kingston: MQUP.

Cox, F. (2009). Human rights and the mandatory detention of children seeking refugee status: Australia changes its policy. *International Law News*, pp. 14–.

Creese, G. and Wiebe, B. (2012). 'Survival Employment': Gender and Deskilling among African Immigrants in Canada: *Survival Employment. International Migration,* 50(5), 56–76. https://doi.org/10.1111/j.1468-2435.2009.00531.x.

Crenshaw, K. W. (1989). Demarginalizing the Intersection of Race and Sex: A Black Feminist Critique of Antidiscrimination Doctrine, Feminist Theory and Antiracist Politics. *University of Chicago Legal Forum*, pp. 139–167.

Crivello, G. (2009). *"Becoming somebody": Youth Transitions through Education and Migration—Evidence from Young Lives, Peru*. Oxford: Young Lives.

Crock, M. and Martin, H. (2018). First things first: international law and the protection of migrant children. In: L. Benson, ed.,

Protecting Migrant Children: In Search of Best Practice. Edward Elgar Publishing, pp. 75–96. Available at: http://www.elgaronline.com/view/edcoll/9781786430250/9781786430250.00013.xml (Accessed June 2, 2020).

Cunningham, H. (1995). *Children and Childhood in Western Society since 1500.* Studies in modern history (Longman). London and New York: Longman.

CWICE and JIAS (2022). Unaccompanied and Separated Children Under CUAET: A call to position Canada as Best in Class Leader in the protection and welfare of children & youth. Available at: https://www.cwice.ca/docs/default-source/cwice/uasc-under-cuaet-report.pdf?sfvrsn=649b1fb3_5.

Dauvergne, C. and Millbank, J. (2011). Forced Marriage and Refugee Status. Available at: https://www.refworld.org/reference/countryrep/asylumaid/2011/en/78899.

Deneva, N. (2017). Flexible kin work, flexible migration: Aging migrants caught between productive and reproductive labour in the European Union. In: *Transnational Aging and Reconfigurations of Kin Work.* New Brunswick: Rutgers University Press, pp. 25–42.

Deng, S. A. and Marlowe, J. M. (2013). Refugee Resettlement and Parenting in a Different Context. *Journal of Immigrant & Refugee Studies,* 11(4), pp. 416–430.

Denov, M. S., Mitchell, C. and Rabiau, M. eds. (2023). *Global Child: Children and Families Affected by War, Displacement and Migration.* Genocide, political violence, human rights series. New Brunswick: Rutgers University Press.

Dossa, P. A. (2020). *Social Palliation: Canadian Muslims' Storied Lives on Living and Dying.* Toronto, Buffalo, and London: University of Toronto Press.

Dossa, P. A. and Coe, C. (2017). Introduction: Transnational aging and reconfigurations of kin work. In: *Transnational Aging and Reconfigurations of Kin Work.* New Brunswick: Rutgers University Press.

Dryden-Peterson, S. (2016). Refugee Education in Countries of First Asylum: Breaking Open the Black Box of Pre-resettlement Experiences. *Theory and Research in Education*, 14(2), pp. 131–148. Available at: https://doi.org/10.1177/1477878515622703.

Dubus, N. (2010). "I feel like her daughter not her mother": Ethnographic Trans-cultural Perspective of the Experiences of Aging for a Group of Southeast Asian Refugees in the United States. *Journal of Aging Studies*, 24(3), pp. 204–211. Available at: https://doi.org/10.1016/j.jaging.2010.02.002.

Dubus, N. (2018). Arriving Old: A Qualitative Study of Elder Refugee Women's Self-perceptions of the First Year of Resettlement. *Journal of Gerontological Social Work*, 61(4), pp. 393–410. Available at: https://doi.org/10.1080/01634 372.2018.1457124.

Ducke, E. and Riabenko, E. (2024). Forced to relive childhood horrors in old age. *New York Times*, May 20. Available at: https://www. nytimes.com/2024/05/20/world/europe/ukrainian-nazi-russian-occupation-survivors.html.

Dunton, E. S. (2012). Same Sex, Different Rights: Amending U.S. Immigration Law to Recognize Same-Sex Partners of Refugees and Asylees. *Family Court Review*, 50(2), pp. 357–371. Available at: https://doi.org/10.1111/j.1744-1617.2012.01441.x.

Durieux, J.-F. (2008). The Many Faces of "Prima Facie": Group-Based Evidence in Refugee Status Determination. *Refuge: Canada's Journal on Refugees*, 25(2), pp. 151–163. Available at: https://doi. org/10.25071/1920-7336.26037.

Ealom, J. (2022). The long way home. *Toronto Life*, July 25. Available at: https://torontolife.com/memoir/how-i-escaped-from-manus-prison-a-memoir/.

Elnakib, S. *et al.* (2021). Child Marriage among Somali Refugees in Ethiopia: A Cross Sectional Survey of Adolescent Girls and Adult Women. *BMC Public Health*, 21(1), p. 1051. Available at: https:// doi.org/10.1186/s12889-021-11080-5.

Euro-Med Human Rights Monitor (2023). "Happiness, Love and Understanding": The Protection of Unaccompanied Minors in the 27 EU Member States. Available at: https://reliefweb.int/report/austria/happiness-love-and-understanding-protection-unaccompanied-minors-27-eu-member-states-enar.

Febria, M. and Jones, T. (2023). Going the Distance: Immigrant Youth in Canada's Labour Market. World Education Services. Available at: https://eric.ed.gov/?id=ED628407.

Fee, M. (2022). Lives Stalled: The Costs of Waiting for Refugee Resettlement. *Journal of Ethnic and Migration Studies*, 48(11), pp. 2659–2677. Available at: https://doi.org/10.1080/1369183X.2021.1876554.

Fiddian-Qasmiyeh, E. (2014). *The Ideal Refugees: Gender, Islam, and the Sahrawi Politics of Survival*. 1st edn. Gender, culture, and politics in the Middle East. Syracuse, New York: Syracuse University Press.

FitzGerald, D. S. (2019). *Refuge beyond Reach: How Rich Democracies Repel Asylum Seekers*. Oxford: Oxford University Press.

Flynn, M. and Wong, L. (2022). Older Migrants and Overcoming Employment Barriers: Does Community Activism Provide the Answer? *Frontiers in Sociology*, 7, p. 845623. Available at: https://doi.org/10.3389/fsoc.2022.845623.

Friends Committee on National Legislation (n.d.). Sadhana Singh, 31—Spring Lobby Weekend 2018 Participant. Available at: https://www.fcnl.org/people/sadhana-singh-31.

Gambaro, L., Neidhöfer, G. and Spiess, C. K. (2021). The Effect of Early Childhood Education and Care Services on the Integration of Refugee Families. *Labour Economics*, 72, p. 102053. Available at: https://doi.org/10.1016/j.labeco.2021.102053.

Gardner, K. (2009). Lives in Motion: The Life-Course, Movement and Migration in Bangladesh. *Journal of South Asian Development*, 4(2), pp. 229–251. Available at: https://doi.org/10.1177/097317410900400204.

Gardner, K. (2021). *Age, Narrative and Migration: The Life Course and Life Histories of Bengali Elders in London*. First issued in paperback. London and New York: Routledge.

Gaucher, M. (2018). *A Family Matter: Citizenship, Conjugal Relationships, and Canadian Immigration Policy*. Vancouver and Toronto: UBC Press.

Gautam, R., Mawn, B. E. and Beehler, S. (2018). Bhutanese Older Adult Refugees Recently Resettled in the United States: A Better Life with Little Sorrows. *Journal of Transcultural Nursing*, 29(2), pp. 165–171. Available at: https://doi.org/10.1177/104365961 7696975.

Ghebrai, S. and Ballucci, D. (2022). The Social Construction of Age and "Best Interests" Discourses: An Intersectional Analysis of Canadian Immigration and Refugee Policy for Children. *Journal of Refugee Studies*, 35(3), pp. 1143–1159. Available at: https://doi.org/10.1093/jrs/feac039.

Giele, J. and Elder, G. (1998). *Methods of Life Course Research: Qualitative and Quantitative Approaches*. Thousand Oaks, CA: Sage. Available at: https://doi.org/10.4135/978148 3348919.

Gonzales, R. G. (2016). *Lives in Limbo: Undocumented and Coming of Age in America*. Oakland, CA: University of California Press.

Gonzales, R. G. *et al.* (2018). (Un)authorized Transitions: Illegality, DACA, and the Life Course. *Research in Human Development*, 15(3–4), pp. 345–359. Available at: https://doi.org/10.1080/15427 609.2018.1502543.

Gonzales, R. G., & Chavez, L. R. (2012). "Awakening to a nightmare" Abjectivity and illegality in the lives of undocumented 1.5-generation Latino immigrants in the United States. Current Anthropology, 53(3), 255–268.

Government of the United Kingdom (n.d.). Claim asylum in the UK. Available at: https://www.gov.uk/claim-asylum/eligibility.

Grabska, K. (2020). "Wasting time": Migratory Trajectories of Adolescence among Eritrean Refugee Girls in Khartoum. *Critical African Studies*, 12(1), pp. 22–36.

Grabska, K., Regt, M. de and Franco, N. D. (2018). *Adolescent Girls' Migration in The Global South: Transitions into Adulthood*. New York: Springer.

Grace, B. L. (2019). Family from Afar? Transnationalism and Refugee Extended Families after Resettlement. *Journal of Refugee Studies*, 32(1), pp. 125–143. Available at: https://doi.org/10.1093/jrs/fey019.

Griffiths, M. B. E. (2014). Out of Time: The Temporal Uncertainties of Refused Asylum Seekers and Immigration Detainees. *Journal of Ethnic and Migration Studies*, 40(12), pp. 1991–2009. Available at: https://doi.org/10.1080/1369183X.2014.907737.

Grønseth, A. S. (2018). Migrating Rituals: Negotiations of Belonging and Otherness among Tamils in Norway. *Journal of Ethnic and Migration Studies*, 44(16), pp. 2617–2633. Available at: https://doi.org/10.1080/1369183X.2017.1389026.

Guo, S. (2009). Difference, Deficiency, and Devaulation: Tracing the Roots of Non-Recognition of Foreign Credentials for Immigrant Professionals in Canada. *Canadian Journal for the Study of Adult Education* 22(1), pp. 37–52.

Guo, Y., Maitra, S. and Guo, S. (2019). "I Belong to Nowhere": Syrian Refugee Children's Perspectives on School Integration. *Journal of Contemporary Issues in Education*, 14(1). Available at: https://doi.org/10.20355/jcie29362.

Guruge, S. *et al.* (2021). Elder Abuse Risk Factors: Perceptions among Older Chinese, Korean, Punjabi, and Tamil Immigrants in Toronto. *Journal of Migration and Health*, 4, p. 100059. Available at: https://doi.org/10.1016/j.jmh.2021.100059.

Halabi, N. (2023). Personal communication.

Halpert, M. (2023). "Like a kidnapping": Migrant family separated under Trump reunited after four years. *BBC News*, May 8. Available at: https://www.bbc.com/news/world-us-canada-64959802.

Harrell-Bond, B. E. and Wilson, K. B. (1990). Dealing with Dying: Some Anthropological Reflections on the Need for Assistance by Refugee Relief Programmes for Bereavement and Burial. *Journal of Refugee Studies*, 3(3), pp. 228–243. Available at: https://doi.org/10.1093/jrs/3.3.228.

Hasager, L. (2024). Does Granting Refugee Status to Family-Reunified Women Improve their Integration?. *Journal of Public Economics*, 234, pp. 105–119.

HelpAge International (2023a). "Everyone has their own story, but it hurts us all the same" Learning from the experiences of older Ukrainian refugees in Poland. Available at: https://reliefweb.int/report/poland/everyone-has-their-own-story-it-hurts-us-all-same-learning-experiences-older-ukrainian-refugees-poland-enpl#:~:text=Poland%20saw%20one%20of%20the,over%2060%20years%20of%20age.

HelpAge International (2023b). "I've lost the life I knew": Older people's experiences of the Ukraine war and their inclusion in the humanitarian response. Available at: https://www.helpage.org/silo/files/ive-lost-the-life-i-knewolder-peoples-experiences-of-the-ukraine-warreport.pdf.

HelpAge International (2024a). Life finds a way: resolve and resilience of older people in Ukraine. February 21. Available at: https://www.helpage.org/story/life-finds-a-way-resolve-and-resilience-of-older-people-in-ukraine/.

HelpAge International (2024b). Two years of war in Ukraine through the eyes of older people. Available at: https://www.helpage.org/two-years-of-war-in-ukraine/.

Hirsch, S. (2019). Racism, "second generation" Refugees and the Asylum System. *Identities*, 26(1), pp. 88–106. Available at: https://doi.org/10.1080/1070289X.2017.1361263.

Hodes, M. and Vostanis, P. (2019). Practitioner Review: Mental Health Problems of Refugee Children and Adolescents and Their Management. *Journal of Child Psychology and Psychiatry*, 60(7), pp. 716–731. Available at: https://doi.org/10.1111/jcpp.13002.

Horn, V. and Fokkema, T. (2023). Drivers of Loneliness among Older Refugees. *Journal of Refugee Studies*, fead027. Available at: https://doi.org/10.1093/jrs/fead027.

Hugman, R., Bartolomei, L. and Pittaway, E. (2004). It Is Part of Your Life until You Die: Older Refugees in Australia. *Australasian Journal on Ageing*, 23(3), pp. 147–149. Available at: https://doi.org/10.1111/j.1741-6612.2004.00037.x.

Hyndman, J. (2010). Introduction: The Feminist Politics of Refugee Migration. *Gender, Place & Culture*, 17(4), pp. 453–459. Available at: https://doi.org/10.1080/0966369X.2010.485835.

Hynie, M., Guruge, S. and Shakya, Y. B. (2013). Family Relationships of Afghan, Karen and Sudanese Refugee Youth. *Canadian Ethnic Studies*, 44(3), pp. 11–28. Available at: https://doi.org/10.1353/ces.2013.0011.

IHRC, N. (2015). Registering rights: Syrian refugees and the documentation of births, marriages, and deaths in Jordan. Available at: http://hrp.law.harvard.edu/wp-content/uploads/2015/11/Registering-rights-report-NRC-IHRC-October2015.pdf.

Immigration and Refugee Board Canada (2023). Chairperson's Guideline 3: Proceedings Involving Minors at the Immigration and Refugee Board. Available at: https://irb-cisr.gc.ca/en/legal-policy/policies/Pages/GuideDir03-2023.aspx.

Immigration, Refugees and Citizenship Canada. (2018). Processing family members as part of a resettlement sponsorship application. Available at: https://www.canada.ca/en/immigration-refugees-citizenship/corporate/publications-manuals/operational-bulletins-manuals/refugee-protection/resettlement/eligibility/determining-which-family-members-eligible-resettlement.html (Accessed February 23, 2024).

Islam, M. M., Khan, M. N. and Rahman, M. M. (2021). Factors Affecting Child Marriage and Contraceptive Use among Rohingya Girls in Refugee Camps. *The Lancet Regional Health—Western Pacific*, 12, p. 100175. Available at: https://doi.org/10.1016/j.lan wpc.2021.100175.

Jackson, S. and Bauder, H. (2014). Neither Temporary, Nor Permanent: The Precarious Employment Experiences of Refugee Claimants in Canada. *Journal of Refugee Studies*, 27(3), 360–81. Available at: https://doi.org/10.1093/jrs/fet048.

James, A. *et al.* (1998). Theorizing Childhood. *Sociology*, 32(4), pp. 888–891.

Kaga, M. and Nakache, D. (2019). Whose Needs Count in Situations of Forced Displacement Revaluing Older People and Addressing Their Exclusion from Research and Humanitarian Programmes. *International Journal of Migration and Border Studies*, 5(1/2), p. 134. Available at: https://doi.org/10.1504/IJMBS.2019.099723.

Kahil, R., Iqbal, M. and Maghbouleh, N. (2022). Grandmothers Behind the Scenes: Subordinate Integration, Care Work, and Power in Syrian Canadian Refugee Resettlement. *Refuge: Canada's Journal on Refugees*, 38(2), pp. 1–18. Available at: https://doi.org/10.25071/1920-7336.40937.

Kassam, A. (2017). Syrian refugee gives birth in Canada—after secretly entering labour en route. *Guardian*, February 2. Available at: https://www.theguardian.com/world/2017/feb/02/canada-syria-refugee-birth-ibtesam-alkarnake.

Kelly, A. (2024). "They are trying to eradicate us completely": the passion and pain of telling the stories of Afghan women. *Guardian*, May 2. Available at: https://www.theguardian.com/global-development/2024/may/02/they-are-trying-to-eradicate-us-completely-the-passion-and-pain-of-telling-the-stories-of-afg han-women.

Khuri, J. *et al.* (2022). Dietary Intake and Nutritional Status among Refugees in Host Countries: A Systematic Review. *Advances in*

Nutrition, 13(5), pp. 1846–1865. Available at: https://doi.org/10.1093/advances/nmac051.

Kirkendall, A. and Dutt, A. (2023). Refugee Women's Pregnancy and Childbirth Experiences in the US: Examining Context through a Reproductive Justice Framework. *Feminism & Psychology*, p. 095935352211491. Available at: https://doi.org/10.1177/09593535221149166.

Kronick, R., Rousseau, C. and Cleveland, J. (2018). Refugee Children's Sandplay Narratives in Immigration Detention in Canada. *European Child & Adolescent Psychiatry*, 27(4), pp. 423–437. Available at: https://doi.org/10.1007/s00787-017-1012-0.

Kulu, H. and Milewski, N. (2007). Family Change and Migration in the Life Course. *Demographic Research*, 17, pp. 567–590.

Lamb, C. S. (2020). Constructing Early Childhood Services as Culturally Credible Trauma-recovery Environments: Participatory Barriers and Eenablers for Refugee Families. *European Early Childhood Education Research Journal*, 28(1), pp. 129–148. Available at: https://doi.org/10.1080/1350293X.2020.1707368.

Lamba, N. K. (2008). The Employment Experiences of Canadian Refugees: Measuring the Impact of Human and Social Capital on Quality of Employment*. *Canadian Review of Sociology/Revue Canadienne de Sociologie*, 40(1), 45–64. Available at: https://doi.org/10.1111/j.1755-618X.2003.tb00235.x.

Le Gall, J. and Rachédi, L. (2019). The emotional costs of being unable to attend the funeral of a relative in one's country of origin. In: *Transnational Death*, pp. 65–81.

Leclerc, G. and Shreeves, R. (2023). Women's rights in Afghanistan: An ongoing battle. European Parliamentary Research Service. Available at: https://www.europarl.europa.eu/RegData/etudes/BRIE/2023/747084/EPRS_BRI(2023)747084_EN.pdf.

Lee, E. S., Szkudlarek, B., Nguyen, D. C. and Nardon, L. (2020). Unveiling the *Canvas Ceiling*: A Multidisciplinary Literature

Review of Refugee Employment and Workforce Integration. *International Journal of Management Reviews* 22(2), pp. 193–216. Available at: https://doi.org/10.1111/ijmr.12222.

Lindley, A. (2009). The Early-Morning Phonecall: Remittances from a Refugee Diaspora Perspective. *Journal of Ethnic and Migration Studies*, 35(8), pp. 1315–1334. Available at: https://doi. org/10.1080/13691830903123112.

Lundberg, A. (2011). The Best Interests of the Child Principle in Swedish Asylum Cases: The Marginalization of Children's Rights. *Journal of Human Rights Practice*, 3(1), pp. 49–70. Available at: https://doi.org/10.1093/jhuman/hur002.

Madi, F. *et al.* (2019). Death, Dying, and End-of-Life Experiences Among Refugees: A Scoping Review. *Journal of Palliative Care*, 34(2), pp. 139–144. Available at: https://doi.org/10.1177/08258 59718812770.

Madziva, R. (2016). Transnational Parenthood and Forced Migration: The Case of Asylum-seeking Parents who are Forcibly Separated from their Families by Immigration Laws. *Families, Relationships and Societies*, 5(2), pp. 281–297. Available at: https:// doi.org/10.1332/204674315X14479281723965.

Maguire, S. (2012). Putting Adolescents and Youth at the Centre. *Forced Migration Review*, 40. Available at: https://www.fmreview. org/young-and-out-of-place/maguire.

Maheen, H. *et al.* (2021). Sexual and Reproductive Health Service Utilisation of Adolescents and Young People from Migrant and Refugee Backgrounds in High-income Settings: A Qualitative Evidence Synthesis (QES). *Sexual Health*, 18(4), pp. 283–293. Available at: https://doi.org/10.1071/SH20112.

Marshall, N. (2021). Queering Cyc Praxis: What I Learned from LGBTQI+ Newcomer, Refugee, and Immigrant Student Experiences in Canada. *International Journal of Child, Youth and Family Studies*, 12(3–4), pp. 170–202. Available at: https://doi.org/ 10.18357/ijcyfs123-4202120344.

Mayall, B. (2002). *Towards a Sociology for Childhood: Thinking from Children's Lives*. Buckingham, PA: Open University Press.

McKee, C. *et al.* (2019). Fostering Better Integration Through Youth-Led Refugee Sponsorship. *Refuge*, 35(2), pp. 74–85. Available at: https://doi.org/10.7202/1064821ar.

McLaughlin, C. (2017). "They don't look like children": Child Asylum-seekers, the Dubs Amendment and the Politics of Childhood. *Journal of Ethnic and Migration Studies*, pp. 1–17. Available at: https://doi.org/10.1080/1369183X.2017.1417027.

McMichael, C., Gifford, S. M. and Correa-Velez, I. (2011). Negotiating Family, Navigating Resettlement: Family Connectedness amongst Resettled Youth with Refugee Backgrounds Living in Melbourne, Australia. *Journal of Youth Studies*, 14(2), pp. 179–195. Available at: https://doi.org/10.1080/13676261.2010.506529.

Migration Policy Institute (2019). Profile of the Unauthorized Population: United States. Available at: https://www.migratio npolicy.org/data/unauthorized-immigrant-population/state/US.

Milton, A. *et al.* (2017). Trapped in Statelessness: Rohingya Refugees in Bangladesh. *International Journal of Environmental Research and Public Health*, 14(8), p. 942. Available at: https://doi. org/10.3390/ijerph14080942.

Moinolnolki, N. and Han, M. (2017). No Child Left Behind: What About Refugees?. *Childhood Education*, 93(1), pp. 3–9. Available at: https://doi.org/10.1080/00094056.2017.1275231.

Mölsä, M. *et al.* (2017). Mental Health among Older Refugees: The Role of Trauma, Discrimination, and Religiousness. *Aging & Mental Health*, 21(8), pp. 829–837. Available at: https://doi.org/10.1080/13607863.2016.1165183.

Morales, A., Yakushko, O. F. and Castro, A. J. (2012). Language Brokering Among Mexican-Immigrant Families in the Midwest: A Multiple Case Study. *The Counseling Psychologist*, 40(4), pp. 520–553. Available at: https://doi.org/10.1177/0011000011417312.

Morales, F. R. *et al.* (2022). Humanitarian Crisis on the US–Mexico Border: Mental Health Needs of Refugees and Asylum Seekers. *Current Opinion in Psychology*, 48, p. 101452. Available at: https://doi.org/10.1016/j.copsyc.2022.101452.

Morantz, G., Rousseau, C. and Heymann, J. (2012). The Divergent Experiences of Children and Adults in the Relocation Process: Perspectives of Child and Parent Refugee Claimants in Montreal. *Journal of Refugee Studies*, 25(1), pp. 71–92. Available at: https://doi.org/10.1093/jrs/fer025.

Morrison-Beedy, D. *et al.* (2022). Protecting Their Daughters with Knowledge: Understanding Refugee Parental Consent for a U.S.-Based Teen Sexual Health Program. *American Journal of Sexuality Education*, 17(4), pp. 474–489. Available at: https://doi.org/10.1080/15546128.2022.2052217.

My Lives of Uncertainty: Sadhana Singh at TEDxWilliam&Mary (2018). Available at: https://discover.trinitydc.edu/connect/2018/04/29/my-lives-of-uncertainty-sadhana-singh-at-tedxwilliammary/.

Neikirk, A. M. (2018). A Moral Marriage: Humanitarian Values and the Bhutanese Refugees. *Journal of Refugee Studies*, 31(1), pp. 63–81. Available at: https://doi.org/10.1093/jrs/fex015.

Ní Laoire, C. (2023). Young people, intergenerationality and the familial reproduction of transnational migrations and immobilities. In: J. Waters and B. Yeoh, eds., *Handbook on Migration and the Family*. Edward Elgar Publishing, pp. 118–134. Available at: https://doi.org/10.4337/9781789908732.00014.

Nibbs, F. G. (2014). *Belonging: The Social Dynamics of Fitting In as Experienced by Hmong Refugees in Germany and Texas*. European anthropology series. Durham, NC: Carolina Academic Press.

Nichols, L., Ha, B. and Tyyskä, V. (2019). Canadian Immigrant Youth and the Education-Employment Nexus. *Canadian Journal of Family and Youth / Le Journal Canadien de Famille et de la Jeunesse*, 12(1), pp. 178–199. Available at: https://doi.org/10.29173/cjfy29497.

Nicholson, E. (2022). Ukrainian Holocaust survivors flee war again — this time to Germany. NPR. April 2022. Available at: https://www.npr.org/2022/04/12/1092289301/germany-ber lin-ukraine-holocaust-survivors

Nielsen, D. S. et al. (2018). "Caught in a Generation Gap": A Generation Perspective on Refugees Getting Old in Denmark—A Qualitative Study. Journal of Transcultural Nursing, 29(3), pp. 265–273. Available at: https://doi.org/10.1177/1043659617718064.

Nolin, C. (2020). Transnational Ruptures: Gender and Forced Migration. London: Routledge.

Noll, G. (2016). Junk Science? Four Arguments against the Radiological Age Assessment of Unaccompanied Minors Seeking Asylum. International Journal of Refugee Law, 28(2), pp. 234–250. Available at: https://doi.org/10.1093/ijrl/eew020.

Noori, S. (2020). Living within hyphenated paradoxes—The canadian adolescent refugee experience. PhD thesis. York University. Available at: http://hdl.handle.net/10315/37981.

Nur, H. A. et al. (2021). A Scoping Review and Assessing the Evidence for Nutrition Education Delivery Strategies for Refugees in High-Income Countries. Advances in Nutrition, 12(6), pp. 2508–2524. Available at: https://doi.org/10.1093/advances/nmab080.

Oberoi, A. K. (2016). Mentoring for first-generation immigrant and refugee youth. National Mentoring Resource Center. Available at: https://nightingalementoring.mau.se/files/2019/09/ImmigrantRefugeeYouth_Population_Review.pdf.

Omar, I. and Paley, R. (2020). This is What America Looks Like: My Journey from Refugee to Congresswoman. 1st edn. New York: Dey Street.

Orgocka, A. and Clark-Kazak, C. (eds.). (2012). Independent Child Migrations: Insights into Agency, Vulnerability, and Structure. John Wiley & Sons.

Parmar, P. K. *et al.* (2019). Mortality in Rohingya Refugee Camps in Bangladesh: Historical, Social, and Political Context. *Sexual and Reproductive Health Matters*, 27(2), pp. 39–49. Available at: https://doi.org/10.1080/26410397.2019.1610275.

Perreira, K. M., Harris, K. M. and Lee, D. (2007). Immigrant Youth in the Labor Market. *Work and Occupations*, 34(1), pp. 5–34. Available at: https://doi.org/10.1177/0730888406295394.

Phillimore, J. and Cheung, S. Y. (2021). The Violence of Uncertainty: Empirical Evidence on How Asylum Waiting Time Undermines Refugee Health. *Social Science & Medicine*, 282, p. 114154. Available at: https://doi.org/10.1016/j.socscimed.2021.114154.

Ploeg, J., Lohfeld, L. and Walsh, C. A. (2013). What Is "Elder Abuse"? Voices From the Margin: The Views of Underrepresented Canadian Older Adults. *Journal of Elder Abuse & Neglect*, 25(5), pp. 396–424. Available at: https://doi.org/10.1080/08946566.2013.780956.

Pobjoy, J. M. (2017). *The Child in International Refugee Law*. Cambridge, UK: Cambridge University Press.

Portes, A. and MacLeod, D. (1996). What Shall I Call Myself? Hispanic Identity Formation in the Second Generation. *Ethnic and Racial Studies*, 19(3), pp. 523–547. Available at: https://doi.org/10.1080/01419870.1996.9993923.

Poureslami, I. *et al.* (2013). Bridging Immigrants and Refugees with Early Childhood Development Services: Partnership Research in the Ddevelopment of an Effective Service Model. *Early Child Development and Care*, 183(12), pp. 1924–1942. Available at: https://doi.org/10.1080/03004430.2013.763252.

Puig, M. E. (2002). The Adultification of Refugee Children: Implications for Cross-Cultural Social Work Practice. *Journal of Human Behavior in the Social Environment*, 5(3–4), pp. 85–95. Available at: https://doi.org/10.1300/J137v05n03_05.

Quek, K. (2018). *Marriage Trafficking: Women in Forced Wedlock.* Routledge studies in gender and global politics. London and New York: Routledge.

Rap, S. (2022). "A Test that is about Your Life": The Involvement of Refugee Children in Asylum Application Proceedings in the Netherlands. *Refugee Survey Quarterly*, 41(2), pp. 298–319. Available at: https://doi.org/10.1093/rsq/hdac004.

RetroReport (2022). Holocaust survivors fleeing Ukraine find a new home in Germany. September 9. Available at: https://retr oreport.org/video/holocaust-survivors-fleeing-ukraine-find-a-new-home-in-germany/.

Rogoff, B. (1991). *Apprenticeship in Thinking: Cognitive Development in Social Context.* New York: Oxford University Press.

Secor-Turner, M. *et al.* (2021). Adapting Evidence-Based Sexuality Education to Meet the Needs of Refugee Youth in the USA. *American Journal of Sexuality Education*, 16(4), pp. 518–532. Available at: https://doi.org/10.1080/15546128.2021.1953659.

Seibel, K. (2016a). Bureaucratic Birthdates: Chronometric Old Age as Resource and Liability in U.S. Refugee Resettlement. *Refuge: Canada's Journal on Refugees*, 32(3), pp. 8–17. Available at: https://doi.org/10.25071/1920-7336.40347.

Seibel, K. (2016b). *Unsettling age: Constructions of later life and support in US resettlement bureaucracy.* PhD thesis. Northwestern University.

Shakhsari, S. (2014). The Queer Time of Death: Temporality, Geopolitics, and Refugee Rights. *Sexualities*, 17(8), pp. 998–1015. Available at: https://doi.org/10.1177/1363460714552261.

Shakya, Y. B. *et al.* (2014). Newcomer refugee youth as "resettlement champions" for their families: Vulnerability, resilience and empowerment. In: *Refuge and Resilience.* International Perspectives on Migration. Dordrecht: Springer, pp. 131–154. Available at: https://doi.org/10.1007/978-94-007-7923-5_9.

Shanneik, Y. (2021). Displacement, Humanitarian Interventions and Gender Rights in the Middle East: Syrian Refugees in Jordan as a Case Study. *Journal of Ethnic and Migration Studies*, 47(15), pp. 3329–3344. Available at: https://doi.org/10.1080/13691 83X.2021.1926944.

Silverman, S. (2016). "Imposter-Children" in the UK Refugee Status Determination Process. *Refuge*, 32(3), p. 30.

Silverman, S. J. (2024). Immigration Detention in Canada: Concepts and Controversies. In: *Forced Migration in/to Canada: From Colonization to Refugee Resettlement*. MQUP.

Singleton, D. (2001). Age and Second Language Acquisition. *Annual Review of Applied Linguistics*, 21, pp. 77–89. Available at: https://doi.org/10.1017/S0267190501000058.

Slade, N. and Borovnik, M. (2018). "Ageing out of place": Experiences of Resettlement and Belonging among Older Bhutanese Refugees in New Zealand. *New Zealand Geographer*, 74(2), pp. 101–108. Available at: https://doi.org/10.1111/nzg.12188.

Sleijpen, M. *et al.* (2016). Between Power and Powerlessness: A Meta-ethnography of Sources of Resilience in Young Refugees. *Ethnicity & Health*, 21(2), pp. 158–180. Available at: https://doi.org/10.1080/13557858.2015.1044946.

Smyth, C. (2014). *European Asylum Law and the Rights of the Child*. 1st edn. Routledge. Available at: https://doi.org/10.4324/978020 3797297.

Song, S. (2010). Finding One's Place: Shifting Ethnic Identities of Recent Immigrant Children from China, Haiti and Mexico in the United States. *Ethnic and Racial Studies*, 33(6), pp. 1006–1031. Available at: https://doi.org/10.1080/01419870903121340.

Stermac, L., Elgie, S., Clarke, A. and Dunlap, H. (2012). Academic Experiences of War-Zone Students in Canada. *Journal of Youth Studies*, 15(3), pp. 311–28. Available at: https://doi.org/10.1080/ 13676261.2011.643235.

Stevens, K. E., Siraj, I. and Kong, K. (2023). A Critical Review of the Research Evidence on Early Childhood Education and Care in Refugee Contexts in Low- and Middle-income Countries. *International Journal of Child Care and Education Policy*, 17(1), p. 7. Available at: https://doi.org/10.1186/s40723-023-00109-4.

Stevenson, V. (2023). Stunned faces and heartbreak for migrants heading to Roxham as they learn Canada will likely send them back. *CBC News*, March 25.

Stevenson, V. and Rukavina, S. (2023). Canada suspends deportation of Quebec mother and her 3 kids after UN intervention. *CBC News*, July 10. Available at: https://www.cbc.ca/news/canada/montreal/un-human-rights-deportation-1.6902028.

Stolk, Y., Kaplan, I. and Szwarc, J. (2023). Majority Language Acquisition by Children of Refugee Background: A Review. *International Journal of Inclusive Education*, pp. 1–24. Available at: https://doi.org/10.1080/13603116.2023.2210593.

Sudha, S. and Khadka, N. (2022). A Community Engaged Exploratory Study Investigating the Risk of Elder Abuse and Neglect in Two Refugee Communities in Greensboro, North Carolina. *Journal of Elder Abuse & Neglect*, 34(4), pp. 280–301. Available at: https://doi.org/10.1080/08946566.2022.2114970.

Sypek, S. A. *et al.* (2016). A Holistic Approach to Age Estimation in Refugee children. *Journal of Paediatrics and Child Health*, 52(6), pp. 614–620. Available at: https://doi.org/10.1111/jpc.13174.

Tefera, G. W. (2021). Time and Refugee Migration in Human Geographical Research: A Critical Review. *Geoforum*, 127, pp. 116–119. Available at: https://doi.org/10.1016/j.geoforum.2021.10.005.

Thelen, T. and Coe, C. (2019). Political Belonging through Elderly Care: Temporalities, Representations and Mutuality. *Anthropological Theory*, 19(2), pp. 279–299. Available at: https://doi.org/10.1177/1463499617742833.

Thomas, V. and Beck, T. (2010). Changing the way UNHCR does business? An evaluation of the Age, Gender and Diversity

Mainstreaming Strategy, 2004–2009. UNHCR. Available at: https://www.unhcr.org/media/changing-way-unhcr-does-business-eva luation-age-gender-and-diversity-mainstreaming-strategy.

Thurton, D. (2017). "Hardest decision," says Syrian refugee who waited to land in Canada to give birth. *CBC News*, February 5. Available at: https://www.cbc.ca/news/canada/edmonton/alkarnake-ibtesam-syrian-refugee-pregnant-1.3968209.

Tonui, B. C. and Mitschke, D. B. (2022). "We still keep our culture to stay alive": Acculturation and Adaptation among Resettled Young Adult Refugees from Burma. *Journal of Ethnic & Cultural Diversity in Social Work*, 31(2), pp. 121–133. Available at: https://doi.org/10.1080/15313204.2020.1827334.

Townsend, M. (2023). Home Office faces legal action over children missing from UK asylum hotels. *Guardian*, June 11. Available at: https://www.theguardian.com/society/2023/jun/11/home-office-faces-legal-action-over-children-missing-from-uk-asylum-hotels.

Triggs, G. (2018). The impact of detention on the health, well-being and development of children: findings from the second National Inquiry into Children in Immigration Detention. In: M. Crock and L. Benson, eds., *Protecting Migrant Children: In Search of Best Practice*. Northampton, MA: Edward Elgar Publishing, pp. 396–419. Available at: http://www.elgaronline.com/view/edc oll/9781786430250/9781786430250.00033.xml (Accessed June 2, 2020).

UK Government (2021). Vulnerable Persons and Vulnerable Children's Resettlement Schemes Factsheet. Available at: https://www.gov.uk/government/publications/uk-resettlement-sche mes-factsheet-march-2021/vulnerable-persons-and-vulnerable-childrens-resettlement-schemes-factsheet-march-2021.

UN Department of Economic and Social Affairs (2019). World Population Ageing 2019. Available at: https://www.un.org/en/development/desa/population/publications/pdf/ageing/WorldPopulationAgeing2019-Highlights.pdf.

UN General Assembly (1981). International Youth Year: Participation, Development, Peace. Available at: https://docume nts-dds-ny.un.org/doc/RESOLUTION/GEN/NR0/406/54/PDF/ NR040654.pdf?OpenElement.

UN General Assembly (1991). United Nations Principles for Older Persons. General Assembly resolution 46/91. Available at: https:// www.ohchr.org/en/instruments-mechanisms/instruments/uni ted-nations-principles-older-persons.

UNHCR (1997). Guidelines on Policies and Procedures in deal-ing with Unaccompanied Children Seeking Asylum. Available at: https://www.unhcr.org/media/guidelines-policies-and-pro cedures-dealing-unaccompanied-children-seeking-asylum.

UNHCR (2017). UNHCR Age, Gender and Diversity— Accountability Report 2016, p. 56.

UNHCR (2018). UNHCR Policy on Age, Gender and Diversity. Available at: https://www.unhcr.org/5aa13c0c7.pdf.

UNHCR (2023a). Born into a refugee life. Available at: https:// www.unhcr.org/refugee-statistics/insights/explainers/children-born-into-refugee-life.html.

UNHCR (2023b). *UNHCR Resettlement Handbook*. Revised. Geneva, Switzerland: UNHCR. Available at: https://www.unhcr.org/reset tlement-handbook/.

UNHCR (n.d.). Education pathways. Available at: https://www. unhcr.org/what-we-do/build-better-futures/education/tertiary-education/education-pathways.

UNHCR & UNICEF (2021). UNHCR and UNICEF: Background Note on Sex Discrimination in Birth Registration. UNHCR. Available at: https://www.refworld.org/docid/60e2d0554.html.

UNHCR, H. (2021). Working with older persons in forced displace-ment. Available at: https://www.refworld.org/policy/opguida nce/unhcr/2021/en/123481.

Van Raemdonck, A. (2023). Syrian Refugee Men in "double wait-hood": Ethnographic Perspectives on Labour and Marriage in Jordan's Border Towns. *Gender, Place & Culture*, 30(5), pp. 692–713. Available at: https://doi.org/10.1080/0966369X.2023.2178390.

VanderPlaat, M., Ramos, H. and Yoshida, Y. (2012). What do Sponsored Parents and Grandparents Contribute? *Canadian Ethnic Studies; Calgary*, 44(3), pp. 79–96.

Vaquera, E., Castañeda, H. and Aranda, E. (2022). Legal and Ethnoracial Consciousness: Perceptions of Immigrant Media Narratives Among the Latino Undocumented 1.5 Generation. *American Behavioral Scientist*, 66(12), pp. 1606–1626. Available at: https://doi.org/10.1177/00027642221083538.

Veraksa, N. and Pramling Samuelsson, I., eds. (2022). *Piaget and Vygotsky in XXI century: Discourse in Early Childhood Education*. Early Childhood Research and Education: An Inter-theoretical Focus. Cham: Springer International Publishing. Available at: https://doi.org/10.1007/978-3-031-05747-2.

Vives, L. (2020). Child Migration in the US and Spain: Towards a Global Border Regime? *International Migration*, 58(6), pp. 29–44. Available at: https://doi.org/10.1111/imig.12704.

Wali, N. and Renzaho, A. M. N. (2018). "Our riches are our family", The Changing Family Dynamics & Social Capital for New Migrant Families in Australia. *PLOS ONE*. Edited by V. Capraro, 13(12), p. e0209421. Available at: https://doi.org/10.1371/journal.pone.0209421.

Wang, C. J. and Hari, A. (2024). Chinese Grand(parenting) Encourages a Re-imagining of Canada's Immigration Regime. *International Migration*, 62(1), pp. 112–125. Available at: https://doi.org/10.1111/imig.13200.

Welfens, N. and Bonjour, S. (2021). Families First? The Mobilization of Family Norms in Refugee Resettlement. *International Political Sociology*, 15(2), pp. 212–231. Available at: https://doi.org/10.1093/ips/olaa022.

Westcott, H. and Robertson, S. (2017). Childcare, Mobility Decisions and "Staggered" Migration. *Migration, Mobility, & Displacement*, 3(1), p. 85. Available at: https://doi.org/10.18357/mmd31201717075.

White, A. (2012). "Every Wednesday I Am Happy": Childhoods in an Irish Asylum Centre: Childhoods in an Irish Asylum Centre. *Population, Space and Place*, 18(3), pp. 314–326. Available at: https://doi.org/10.1002/psp.659.

Wolf, K. (2016). Marriage Migration Versus Family Reunification: How Does the Marriage and Migration History Affect the Timing of First and Second Childbirth Among Turkish Immigrants in Germany?. *European Journal of Population*, 32(5), pp. 731–759. Available at: https://doi.org/10.1007/s10 680-016-9402-4.

Yoshida, Y. and Amoyaw, J. (2020). Transition to Adulthood of Refugee and Immigrant Children in Canada. *Applied Psycholinguistics*, 41(6), pp. 1465–1495. Available at: https://doi.org/10.1017/S0142716420000363.

Zeweri, H. (2024). Reluctant Disclosure: Epistemic Doubt and Ethical Dilemmas in Australian Forced Marriage Prevention Efforts. *Ethnos*, 89(2), pp. 365–382. Available at: https://doi.org/10.1080/00141844.2022.2040564.

Recommended further reading

Dossa, P. and Coe, C. (2017). *Transnational Aging and Reconfigurations of Kin Work*. New Brunswick: Rutgers University Press.

IOM. (2018). Human Rights of Migrant Children. https://publicati ons.iom.int/system/files/pdf/iml_15_en.pdf

UNHRC. (2018). Policy on Age, Gender and Diversity Accountability. https://www.unhcr.org/media/policy-age-gender-and-diversity-accountability-2018

Documentary film (2018). *Journey Beyond Fear*. October 25, 2018; Director: Robyn Hughes; Australia. https://www.journe ybeyondfear.com/

Jaz O'Hara. Podcast. *Reunited after 10 years: The story of Mez and his little brother Josi*. https://podcasts.apple.com/gb/podc ast/51-reunited-after-ten-years-the-story-of-mez-and/id146 8264562?i=1000622935893

Index

49; and immobility, 6; lived experiences of, 78–79; and temporality, 79, 81–83, 84

Ealom, Jaivet, 78–80

early childhood education and care, 20–21, 94

education: primary, 23; post-secondary, 31, 32, 37–38; right to, 13; secondary, 24–25

family: definitions of, 40, 52, 71–72; migration, 5–6, 23; multigenerational, 68–69; planning, 5; reunification, 51–52; separation, 19, 27–28, 42, 69; as support networks, 59–61, 64; transnational, 62, 72–73; unity, 9, 52

forced migration: and birth, 15–20; and childhood, 20–24, 26–28; and death, 64–66; definition of, 5–6; to Global North, 8–9; in Global South, 7; and old age, 55–60; statistics of, 6–7; studies, 85–86; and youth, 24–27

gender: and birth registration, 18; and caregiving, 38; and healthcare, 25; and life course, 14; and refugee status determination, 40, 49–50; and social age, 15, 22, 59, 85; and vulnerability, 52–53

generation: of immigration cohorts, 22–23, 78, 84–85; and parenthood, 41; and

power relations, 73–74, 76; separation of, 74–75; and social age, 84–85; see also: family

Germany: as top country of asylum, 7–8; and early childhood education and care, 21; and detention, 81; and older refugees, 58, 59–60, 62

healthcare: for children, 13; for infants, 20; maternal, 16–17; for young people, 25, 26

HelpAge, 56, 59

infanticization, 59–60, 73

intersectionality, 2–4, 59, 67

International Organization for Migration, 9

Joya, Zahra, 46–47

language: and citizenship, 16; and education, 18–19, 20–21, 24–25; and healthcare access, 17; and older people, 57, 60, 61, 63–64; training, 75

life course: and adult-centricity, 47–48, 53–54; approach, 4–5; decisions, 10, 38–40, 82; events, 11, 32–34, 58; and intergenerational relations, 41, 73; and social age, 2, 14, 22, 41, 85–86; and time, 82–83

liminality, 31, 42–43

older persons: and data gaps, 86; definition of, 55–56; and health, 60, 62; human rights of, 56–57; and immobility, 55; labour of, 63–64; and language acquisition, 63; and loneliness, 59–60

puberty, 4, 24, 25

marriage: and birth registration, 18; definition of, 70; early 32, 40; and forced migration, 39–41; as life course decision, 5, 10, 38, 82; and social age, 4, 41; and transition to adulthood, 31, 39–40

Omar, Ilhan, 67–69

parenthood, 10, 38, 41–42

refugee status determination, 8, 47–50, 52

refugee resettlement: definition of, 7, 15; family relationships in, 40, 51–52, 68–69, 70–72; and older refugees, 61, 64

retirement, 5, 55–56, 63–64

rites of passage, 4, 24, 34, 65–66

Rohingya, 16, 19, 78, 84

Singh, Sadhana, 33–36

statelessness, 19

Syrian refugees: in Australia, 73–74; in Canada, 14–16, 22, 60–61; in Jordan, 18; statistics of, 7

time: and chronological age, 3–5, 55, 79, 82,; and detention, 81; in displacement, 82–84; and liminality, 31–32, 43, 82–83; political value of, 81–82; and social age, 5, 22, 55–56, 62

Ukrainian refugees: demographics of, 53–54; older 57–58, 59, 64–65; statistics, 7

unaccompanied minors, 26–28, 48

United Kingdom: and age assessments, 28; and asylum claim, 46–47, 48, 71, 83; and hostile environment, 8; and immigration detention, 81; and vulnerability, 52, 53–54

United Nations Convention on Refugees, 1951: and refugee definition, 8, 47–48

United Nations Refugee Agency (UNHCR): and family reunification, 51–52; and guidelines for age categories, 9, 53; and older refugees, 58, 59; and resettlement, 7, 68, 79; statistics, 7, 16, 37; and unaccompanied minors, 27

United States: and border with Canada, 81; and Convention on the Rights of the Child, 13; and family separation, 27–28; and older refugees, 60; and refugee resettlement, 7, 68–69, 72; and undocumented people, 8, 32–36

www.ingramcontent.com/pod-product-compliance
Lightning Source LLC
Chambersburg PA
CBHW071748270326
41928CB00013B/2836